PRAISE FOR THE AUTHOR

"Leah is one of the most determined and trustworthy individuals in my life. Leah and I connected at the beginning of both of us starting new entrepreneur journeys and she has overcome so many struggles and business changes since then. Because she is determined and knows her skills she continues to thrive in her business while helping others do the same!"

– Camille Kurtenbach,
Influencer and owner of Positivity Platform

"I have been collaborating with Leah for a couple of years now. She has many creative ideas, takes initiative and doesn't give up when the going gets tough. I highly recommend working with her and look forward to collaborating on many more projects in the future."

– Janet Johnson,
Owner and founder, Janet E Johnson Agency
and Coaching

"Leah is a great business partner to have in your corner. She has vision and can clearly communicate which makes her stand out. She is always asking for feedback to improve her process which shows how much she cares about her work and the people she works with."

– Shinobu Hindert,
Certified Financial Planner and creator of
Empowered Planning

"Leah is truly a force to be reckoned with. She helped me get my site up and running in record time and maximized my functionality for the types of products and services I offer. Her ability to strategize, foresee potential challenges, and manage tight deadlines made all the difference. She was always just an email away when I needed support or had a question."

– Sarah Duran,
CEO and founder of Fruition Initiatives

"Leah is an excellent collaborator and is also very technically solid. Having Leah's knowledge and her strategic advisory expertise is invaluable. Leah is trustworthy and hard working and I enjoy working with her and would highly recommend you collaborate with her!"

– Brenda Stanton,
Founder of Claim Your Worth!®

THE UNSTOPPABLE
Route

THE UNSTOPPABLE
Route

YOUR PROVEN PATH TO SUCCESS, NO MATTER WHAT

LEAH MEYERS

FOREWORD BY JEREMY BROWN

THRONE
PUBLISHING GROUP

ISBN Softcover: 978-1-949550-49-8
Ebook ISBN: 978-1-949550-50-4

Printed in the United States of America.

Cover Design: Heidi Caperton
Lead Writer: Shelley Furtado-Linton
Editor: Marguerite Bonnett
Proofing Editor: Amanda Dahlin
Publishing Manager: Janet Pomeroy

Throne Publishing Group
1601 East 69th St N Suite 306
Sioux Falls, SD 57108
ThronePG.com

DEDICATION

To Nick & Victoria

For always pushing me to be the best I can be – believing in me and us as a family every muddy step of the way. Being your mom is the best adventure – I love all our adventures!

The two of you are the greatest gifts in this life. May you chase everything you desire, seek new adventures always, and live your best life every day!

ACKNOWLEDGMENTS

I'd like to thank family and friends who encouraged me to continue on my path, supported me through the detours, roadblocks, and change of directions I've made these past few years.

Thank you for your unstoppable love and never giving up on me-no matter what!

Much appreciation to the influencers who inspired me, guided me, and lent a helping hand whenever I needed it.

Thank you to the special people in my life who believed in me even when I didn't believe in myself.

TABLE OF CONTENTS

FOREWORD

I remember scrolling through the seemingly endless (and growing) list of UpWork applicants and applications for over two weeks with no luck. I thought my project was so unique, I needed a specialist. I was trying to build out a Kajabi website, needed custom coding executed within the platform, and I needed it done quickly...as in yesterday!

In other words, I was trying to find a needle in a haystack. And UpWork is one massive haystack.

I truly needed the right person, at the right time to help me achieve the results I was aiming for. And I found exactly that in Leah Meyers.

When I came across Leah's application, I distinctly remember thinking, "She's too good to be true!" I also remember thinking that if she works out, she would be an immensely valuable asset to my companies. She had everything you would want in an applicant: a great track record, a high volume of hours worked, and raving reviews.

I decided to hire Leah for one project that quickly turned into two projects, that quickly turned into several projects and now I refer all my customers to her without hesitation.

The more I worked with Leah and learned about her story, I learned just how much of an extraordinary person I have been blessed to find.

Leah has a heart for empowering people to achieve the results they've always wanted. She has all of the strategy, knowledge, and experience to powerfully speak into nearly any circumstance her clients come across. And she has a work ethic second to none that brings everything together and she truly delivers for people.

Unstoppable is the word I use to describe Leah. And if Unstoppable is a word you want to be used to describe yourself, Leah will show you the way. In this book, Leah not only shows you all of her behind the scenes strategies, but she will literally help you make your own road map so you can reach the destination of the success you define for yourself.

Right now, if you want more out of your life, if you know you're capable of more but can't seem to turn the corner, this book is for you and Leah is your guide. As you read her story, I think you'll see your own.

Be inspired by a vision of someone who has gone through so much, overcome it all, and is somehow finding a way to build both a thriving business and a growing family.

After you're done with this book, I think you too will find that Leah could very well be the right person at the right time for you, just as she was for me not too long ago. And no, she's not too good to be true!

I'm so proud of Leah and happy for you that you've found her. Enjoy the book, apply it to your life, and keep moving forward!

JEREMY BROWN
CEO, Throne Publishing Group and StoryWay

NAVIGATING THE JOURNEY

The best journeys include gear that ensures success. Travelers often include maps, food, and safety items to support them on their way.

Much like those add-ons, this journey includes aides that are meant to enhance and strengthen what you discover along the way.

Download the following supplemental material for these chapters at **theunstoppableroute.com**.

- Chapter One: Your "Go-Map" Strategy
- Chapter Two: Plan Your Route to Make it Happen
- Chapter Three: Your Commitment to Success
- Chapter Six: "No" is the New "Yes"

INTRODUCTION

Entrepreneurship takes determination, vision,
and a whole lot of grit!

~ LEAH MEYERS

I cannot remember when I felt more secure or fulfilled. Being able to say that is a victory because many times along the way there were roadblocks, setbacks, and detours that could have derailed me. In those moments, I could have chosen to let situations, experiences, or others' opinions stop me, but instead, each time I faced a struggle, something in me rose up and I pushed through. The difficulties and challenges became the driving force that pushed me forward to another level.

As I look back over the last few years, I see a pattern of challenge, growth, and then freedom. Just like many others, the struggle is what caused me to grow. The truth is, we rarely grow when things are easy or comfortable. I know some of you will not like that statement, but it is true. Those difficult experiences you face may just be what moves you toward success.

Everyone faces difficulties at some time in their lives. Sadly, many people allow those circumstances to completely derail them. I understand that it is not always easy to get up and move on after you get knocked down, but resiliency is a necessary skill set if you want to be an entrepreneur!

When faced with challenges, setbacks, or trouble, sometimes you must think bigger, act smarter, and adjust course.

The difference between "I can do it," and "I hope I can do it," is found at the level of self-confidence. Having a plan, a vision, and knowing your why will go a long way to bolster your belief in yourself.

Entrepreneurship is not for the faint of heart. It takes determination, vision, and a whole lot of grit. I believe that many people have what it takes to make their dream happen, but when something does not go as it should, they throw up their hands in defeat.

That is why I wrote this book, and I am guessing that is why you are here.

You will soon learn my family's love of travel is an important factor in how and why I do what I do. I love envisioning vacations. I love the planning phase. I love the experiences. I have even learned to love the detours, roadblocks, and delays. You see in detours we sometimes get to see things we would not normally get to see. Delays could be an occasion to stop rushing and give ourselves time to breathe. And roadblocks can provide opportunities to shift how we think and change our approach.

In life journeys, we can choose the route we take, and the pace of our trip. We decide what we want to see along the way and how long we will stay when we arrive at our destination. It is all about the vision we create, the step-goals we have along the way, and the celebrations we have when we reach success.

Of course, there are practical things we can do, and my goal in this book is to shed light on the things I learned along the way. My hope is that you will glean insight into your own journey, and come away with success-driven concepts that are applicable in the real-world.

As you move through the book, I encourage you to take time to complete the questions under Examine Your Path and the action steps under *Execute the Route*, at the end of each chapter. Every successful entrepreneur I know has owned their part in their success. No one is going to do the work for you, so do the work!

Whatever road you have been on, this is your opportunity to change the future to an unstoppable route.

LET'S GO!

Part 1

LAUNCHING

THE GET IT DONE ATTITUDE

Mindset shifts come when we look at life with clarity and honesty,
but real transformation takes ruthless honesty and bravery.
Shedding light on what drives life choices, yields big rewards.

~ LEAH MEYERS

YOU CAN

There was a moment in time when I realized I was on a hamster
wheel.

Some of you know what it is like to wake up every day, knowing there is more out there, but feeling like you are never going
to figure out, or experience what that "thing" is.

Many factors had contributed to the frustration and stress I
felt daily, but that is where I found myself. All I could see were
the obstacles. I had felt that before, but this time, instead of
letting those difficulties hold me back, they became the catalyst
I needed to change. At that moment, I decided my attitude was
going to be one of *no* excuses.

An attitude of no excuses is about pushing through when it is not easy or convenient. Look, there are always things in your life that have potential to hold you back. We often stay in not-so-good places because we focus on excuses like, "Now's the wrong time," "I don't have what I need to start," or "What if I fail?" It is easy to get stuck in that kind of reasoning, but the quickest way out of that thinking is to remind yourself you are wasting valuable time instead of gaining traction.

For me, the need to change became critical when I realized my kids were looking up to me and watching the choices I made. I realized then, that someday they would have to make their own pivotal decisions, and I needed to be an example of how to navigate through life choices in meaningful and productive ways.

That realization became my motivation. When I began my journey, I did what many others do… I looked to people I thought had answers. As I dove into what the experts said, I started to see a common theme. What drove them to move forward was facing the roadblocks they experienced. It was eye-opening; roadblocks could propel us forward.

I decided to use my own challenges to push me forward. It began with a dream of what I wanted my future to look like. As I cast that vision, I took time to outline the steps needed for that to happen. Looking back, what I believed was not big enough. At that point in time, I could not imagine the life I live today. Still, it gave me hope and a future to move towards.

When you decide to do something about your current state, you must commit and follow through. Otherwise, nothing changes. Moving towards the future I envisioned was not easy and it took time, but I stayed focused and single-minded by focusing on the reason *why* I was doing it. For me it was the realization that my life was a living lesson for my children.

One of the biggest motivators is knowing your own *why*. Do not skimp on your *why* – it must be important enough to keep you going. Your best chance of success comes when your *why* is bigger than your excuses. Without your *why*, it is too easy to get stuck in stinking thinking and continue making the same choices you are now.

Personal development, especially when it comes from a place of self-examination, is where it starts. The transformation happens in your mindset. It takes ruthless honesty and bravery, but when you shed light on what is driving your life choices, there are big rewards.

One of the principal motivators for me was having a sense of excitement for the next steps. That enthusiasm kept me inspired to keep going. You need to stay motivated, and it must come from *you*. This is personal and, when you identify those things that excite you, there is a greater chance you will not give up.

It is also important to avoid procrastination. Experience has shown me that a procrastination mindset will derail even the best plans. We have all experienced it in some way, but recognizing the danger and not letting it take over your plans to change, is key to success. The opposite of procrastination is empowerment, and that mindset fills you with energy and excitement to move forward.

As you begin to change, others will probably notice. When someone's life changes dramatically, those around them are often taken aback and curious about how the transformation came about. When my life started to change, people began to ask questions. They wanted to know what I was doing differently. It was encouraging to realize they could see the changes.

My circle of friends shifted, too. One of the most powerful changes you can make is surrounding yourself with people who are like-minded and share your inspiration for the future. Being around those types of people will go far to keep you motivated. As my life changed, I surrounded myself with new people who saw me in a new space, with a new attitude.

My kids were part of that journey, too. Since the day they were born, they have been the *why* behind why I do what I do. I have always believed the most important thing we do as parents is to raise healthy, productive adults. The decisions I made then (and still do) are based on what is best for them.

Even though they were always my top priority, they started to notice changes. I had always made time for them, but now I was more purposeful. I had always made sure I was present for them, but now, I made that more of a priority – even when I was working. Make no mistake, your kids see more than you think they do. My life looked different, and it was noticeable to them! My whole family began to see me differently as I developed a no-BS attitude.

LEAVE YOUR EXCUSES HERE

Most transformations stories begin with reflection. We can only judge how far we have come when we look back at where we came from. That is true of my journey, too.

Being a mom – and especially a single mom – played a big role in who I am today. I had my son at nineteen years old and my daughter was born just a few years later. Being a young mom had its challenges. Most nineteen-year-old kids are doing what kids that age do, but I was raising a child and working. It may not be considered an ideal situation, but I learned so much about myself and my strengths through my role as "mom." Besides, being a young mom has advantages too; I will be an empty-nester by the time I am forty!

I love seeing my kids develop into amazing humans. Children take a lot of time and energy, but for me, the up-side is watching them grow into adults. Still, I would be dishonest if I implied there were no challenges. Most parents face difficulties, worries, and struggles; it is part of parenthood. However, raising my kids has been one of the most profound experiences in my life, and I would not be who I am without them in the story.

Raising children provides opportunity to learn many lessons. As a single mom, I think that is especially true. Parenthood includes sacrifices, hurdles, blessings, and joy. We learn a lot about who we are through our kids. My kids are amazing, and it is a blessing to be an influence in their lives, and hopefully instill in them a sense of identity.

Understanding who we are is an important part of how we operate in life. A strong sense of identity drives the choices we make. By contrast, being uncomfortable in our skin, or struggling with self-worth is quite often at the root of most difficult roads we take in life.

There are many things in our world that play a part in forming our identity. The pressure to conform, or fit in, can make kids doubt who they are, or question what they believe. Growing up, I had the same types of influences, and like a lot of young people, I struggled with knowing and valuing who I was.

Without a clear understanding of my identity, the decisions I made, and the way I related to others was impacted. Lack of self-esteem often results in insecurity and can cause us to become overly dependent on others. We look to those around us for our worth, rather than our value coming from within. Looking back, I see how lack of self-worth played out in my life choices early on.

My insecurities led me to walk through three failed relationships. Reflecting on that time in my life, it is clear to me why I connected with those men. I see now why I stayed and what finally got me to leave. Each relationship had good and bad, but I had to look within myself to identify and take ownership of my part in each one of those experiences.

Allowing myself to honestly look at what motivated me, gave me the information I needed to change how I approached life and relationships. I realized the only thing that I could control is me. I had to become emotionally healthy and independent. So, I figured out what that looked like and made the changes I needed to make.

For me, personal transformation came in the form of confidence and independence. The good and bad in my past relationships taught me a lot about myself, but the biggest takeaway was owning my stuff, taking control of my life and decisions, being in my own driver's seat, and leaving the excuses behind. Today, I have financial and personal freedom. I decide how best to spend my time and who I spend it with. When I have free time, I get to do the things that are important to me.

Being "okay" on your own offers great freedom in a relationship, and being "okay" starts with looking in the mirror. In new relationships, being confident, independent, and emotionally healthy allows each person to be their authentic best self. *That* is what I have today in all my relationships.

When I began this journey, one of the first things I started to do was map out what I wanted my life to look like. That vision included financial and family goals. Like many others, I had a lot of excuses for why my goals might not happen. So, I mapped out what it would take to get past them.

For example, one of my goals was to buy a car without financing it. It was a big goal and it took focus to make it happen. I could come up with a lot of excuses that might have derailed me, but I dealt with them and focused on my goal. It was a great feeling to pay cash for a car within six months of setting that goal. When you leave the excuses behind, your accomplishments become so much sweeter. I had accomplished things before, like earning a Career Car with a network marketing company, but that did not mean as much to me as physically handing over the money to pay for a car!

True mindset shifts come when you look at your life with clarity and honesty. Examine where you have been, then decide where you want to be. You do not have to know every step it will take to get there. Start by casting a vision for your best future.

Before I took time to vision cast, I was more reactive. When something happened, I was forced to make decisions in a hurry, and without much thought to the long-term impact of my choices. Being strategic allowed me to make conscious decisions about what I wanted and how I was going to get there.

If you are wondering what the process looks like, here are a few steps to get you started. I like to call this a "GoMap strategy."

BE FORWARD THINKING TO MOVE FROM REACTIVE TO PROACTIVE.

It is also important to start from your present state. Look at the good and bad of where you are right now. Then, determine where you want to be. Create your vision without limits. What is your big dream? Your best life?

BE STRATEGIC TO IDENTIFY NEXT STEPS.

What are the steps or actions you need for that life to happen? Be as specific as you can.

Once you know your action steps, identify any excuses that could prevent this dream or goal from happening. Be thorough. If you do not identify every potential excuse, they can come up later, and keep you from achieving what you set out to.

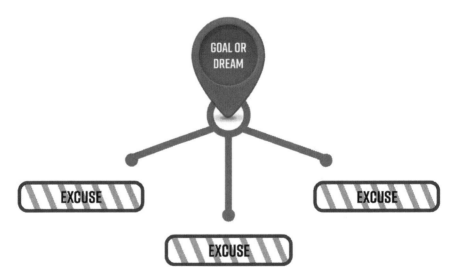

TAKE ACTION.

Identify ways to overcome each excuse. Be specific. Doing this will shift your mindset. Here are some examples:

- I am a single mom, but my kids are watching me.
- I do not have enough money for a new computer (laptop, car, etc.), but I can save for one.
- I do not have enough time, but if I stop binge-watching TV it will free up time.

As you work on this, remember, there is a cost to remaining in your excuses!

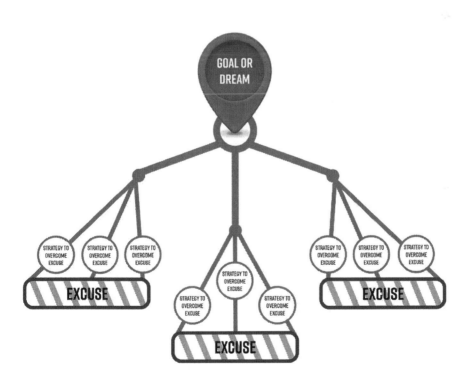

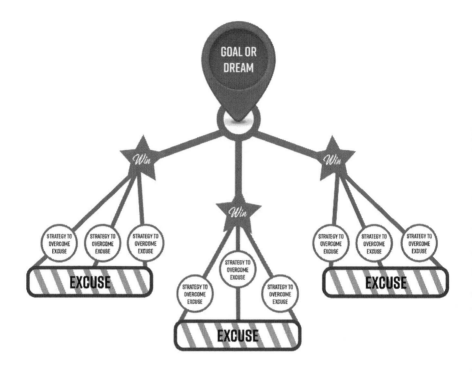

CELEBRATE SUCCESS

Celebrate when you overcome any excuse. This is the most important part of the process. If we only work towards our goals and never celebrate wins, we will become weary and disillusioned. By nature, humans need a reason to change and rewarding yourself is a great way to remain encouraged.

Purchasing the car was my first celebration. My next was taking a trip with my kids when I became financially independent. I kept setting step goals and rewarding myself for each one I accomplished.

Now, it is time for you to make a decision that could change your life forever. You must do it, no one else can. Are you ready?

EXAMINE YOUR PATH

What choices have impacted your
life in negative ways?

What is your *why* for changing your mindset?

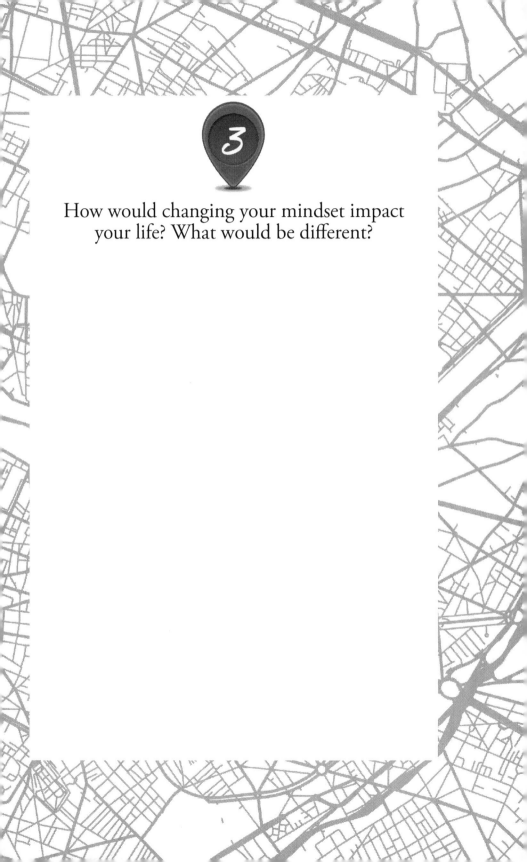

How would changing your mindset impact your life? What would be different?

EXECUTE THE ROUTE

Create your own GoMap strategy.

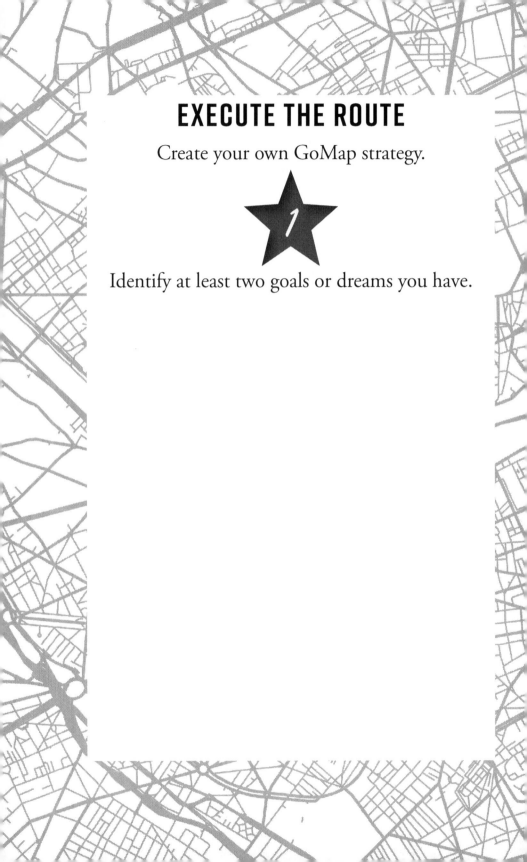

Identify at least two goals or dreams you have.

2

Name the excuses that would stop you from
achieving that dream or goal.

3

Generate at least three strategies for overcoming each excuse.

4

Identify how you will celebrate each win.

MAPPING SUCCESS

Defining your version of success is an intimate process.
Do not get sidetracked by guilt or others people's expectations.

~ LEAH MEYERS

LIFE MAPS

One of my favorite things to do is travel. Although I am fond of every type of travel, there is something quite satisfying about getting behind the wheel of a car and driving. Unlike other modes of travel, driving provides a better view of the world around you. Plus, you can change your route at any time. For me it is almost like a blank piece of paper – you can go anywhere your imagination takes you.

Because I like to drive, I have huge appreciation for maps and GPS. I am all about adventure, but in the end, there is usually a destination, and those tools ensure I am going to end up where I hope to be.

Recently, I made the three-plus hour trip to my parents' home. It is usually a straightforward drive, but on the way back from my visit, we ended up going through three detours. Life can be a lot like that. We may set out in one direction or another, but we can be certain that along the way, we are going to face detours, road closures, pivots, and traffic.

When we begin to envision what our lives can be, it is a bit like creating a life-map. This may not be a *new* analogy, but I believe it fits, because just like the road, life can be an unpredictable, ever growing journey where we get to envision and live out what we dream.

There was a time when our parents and grandparents used paper maps. If you are old enough, you might remember how cumbersome those were. You had to unfold and refold them every time you wanted to recheck your route. In addition, the information was bound by the last printing of the map. If you use an old paper map, you may be missing important and relevant information.

So, for our purpose, I like to picture something more akin to GPS which gives real-time information that is a lot more relevant to current and future needs. Think of the map as the plan and GPS as the navigation system. If this seems confusing, I challenge you to stick with me. I promise, it will start to make sense.

I do not know about you, but when I set out on a trip, especially when I have not been there before, I enter the destination in whatever GPS device I am using, and boom... it gives me several routes that lead to the location. What I love is the option to choose the route that best suits my needs. Maybe I want to take my time and enjoy the trip, so I select the scenic option. Or, maybe I need to get there quickly, so I choose the fastest route.

That is how mapping out a strategy for life works, too. You identify where you want to end up. Then, you choose the best way to get there based on your own wants and needs. What is the bigger-picture goal or vision for your life? What is the life-style, career, financial goal, personal achievement, or life destination you want to achieve? I recommend you allow yourself to dream big in this process. Do not let your current circumstances determine the size of your goal.

The road you take should always begin from where you are in your life right now, but do not get stuck in a one-way-only attitude. Your route should be flexible enough to allow for growth. Be realistic. The direction you choose will help you make decisions and avoid getting trapped in excuses. What is the result you are looking for? What is the larger destination? When you know the answers to these questions, it will help you identify which smaller steps will get you there.

Next, I suggest you map out each "leg" or smaller goal in your journey. When I take a long trip, I usually divide the bigger trip into smaller digestible ones. Doing that helps me stay motivated because long trips can be daunting. It also makes all the details that go into planning long trips more manageable.

Take a moment now and identify the smaller goals you want to accomplish along the way. Here are some examples:

- Improved health or commitment to personal fitness.
- Quality time with family and friends.
- Opportunities to pursue hobbies and passions.
- Freedom to experience adventure.
- Time and resources to travel.
- Better mindset or life balance.

- Time for hobbies or things that bring personal satisfaction.
- Opportunities to contribute to community service or social issues.

Once you make your list, rank them in order of most important to least. Start with the goal at the top of your list. Take a moment now and answer these questions to help you determine the best route to take:

- How does this goal contribute to your overall vision or goal?
- What parts of the vision or goal you named are already in place?
- What parts of the vision or goal you named are still needed?

Close examination of where you currently are in your own life-map, is important. Taking stock allows you to identify what you have, what you need, and what it will take for you to be successful. Many times, we need to dig deep to figure out what is needed, but getting an education, growing a business, becoming a boss, getting a new job, or even changing locations, can fill those empty spots.

The vision you create will help determine the route you choose on your map, and will predict your strategy. The route should reflect the experience you want to have along the way. So, what do you want yours to be?

Fun?

Exciting?

Empowering?

Growing?

Inspiring?

Challenging?

Do not forget to consider the timing needed to reach your goal or vision. Be realistic about where you are and the time you will need to invest in the journey you are taking. Being realistic will help you avoid frustration which could cause you to give up before you get to your goal.

The main thing is, *you* alone get to identify the vision and decide how it will all be put together.

MAKE IT HAPPEN

Use your answers to create a route for that goal. Go back and look at the first goal you listed. Make a list of everything you need for that vision to happen. Pull from the list you create to determine what you will work on each day, and add to your list as you think of things. Prioritize what you can accomplish based on your capacity.

Keep what you write down handy. You will need the map you created to motivate you when you get tired or weary, redirect you when you lose track of where you are going, and to remind you why you are doing what you are doing.

It is okay to work on more than one vision or goal. There are always multiple ways to put your smaller goals together, however, I try to keep the framework in focus. For example, if my main goal is financial freedom, my smaller goals should point towards that as well. The main thing is, *you* get to strategize how you are going to put the map together.

Remember, *this* is a process. You will continue to grow and change, so the map will likely change over time too. Life maps can become whatever you want them to be. They can be as exciting, dream-filled, life-changing, and as limit free, as you want them to be!

As you begin to form your map strategy, remember to remain flexible. Occasionally, GPS will send you down a road that has an unknown detour or dead-end. We have all experienced that and life-maps are no different. Just like GPS in the real world, life sometimes brings the unexpected.

Taking the wrong road happens. I remember a time when I thought I might like to take on a project manager role. I made it work and the project was completed, but it was not a good fit for me! The experience was not my best. I am a strategist and visionary, so project management was not the right road for me. When you find yourself in the wrong place, you must pivot. I could have given up and let myself get stuck because I went the wrong way. In the end, it taught me to keep going and I learned something valuable about myself.

When all the roads are clear and the traffic is flowing, it is easy to enjoy the trip. But like every adventure worth taking, the journey will not always be smooth. Big visions take time, often involve patience, and sometimes require a bit of courage.

Another detour can be comparing yourself to others. Do not get stuck in that trap. Know that your map may not look like anyone else's. In fact, it probably should not. You are unique and that is good. What you offer cannot be provided by anyone else. Remember what it was like when you were a kid? What was your dream then? It is okay to observe where others are going, but always come back to what you really want for *your* life. Make your life-map yours alone.

You also get to decide who comes along on your journey. If you have ever taken a trip with others, you know how important this is! Some individuals may try to put down the choices you make or insist you take a certain route, some may want input on where and when you stop, and others may even try to take over driving. But you alone get to choose which way you go, who gets included, and who does not. Be cautious about who gets a say in your life-map. Do not let yourself get sidetracked by others' expectations or guilt.

Finally, when your map is not making sense or begins to get difficult, I want to encourage you to hang in there. Building a life-map is a process. Struggles are real, but also help you grow. My personal faith tells me that there are always good things that come from difficulties and hurts. As you travel and gain experience, the vision will start to become clear. It is okay if there are roadblock and potholes.

YOUR DEFINITION OF SUCCESS

It is important for us to have our own definition of success. Without it you are apt to be sidetracked by what others say, or what is popular right now. Without an understanding of what success means to you, it can be difficult to know if your goals and vision will drive you towards it.

I define success as a healthy balance of faith, family, career, financial freedom, fun, health, self-care, experiences, and growth or discovery. These are all part of my purpose and each one fuels how I determine my accomplishments. They are not just ideals, they are the beginning, middle, and end of what I do.

Defining your own version of success is an intimate process. It comes from deep within us and looks different for each person. Be intimate enough to know who you are, and give yourself permission to dream about the future and your goals.

What you do, and how you do it will come from how you define success, so do not let anyone else define yours. You can make it whatever you want, but ultimately it is YOU who must do the work. Ownership is yours because you know yourself better than anyone.

Believe and trust in yourself. Think in terms of a map with unlimited options to get you where you want to be. If you had told me back when I was nineteen what my life today would look like, I would have thought you were nuts. The most important thing I can recommend is to give yourself permission to enjoy the journey.

Always look for the silver linings and find joy in the ups and downs of the process. And, never forget to celebrate your accomplishments.

EXAMINE YOUR PATH

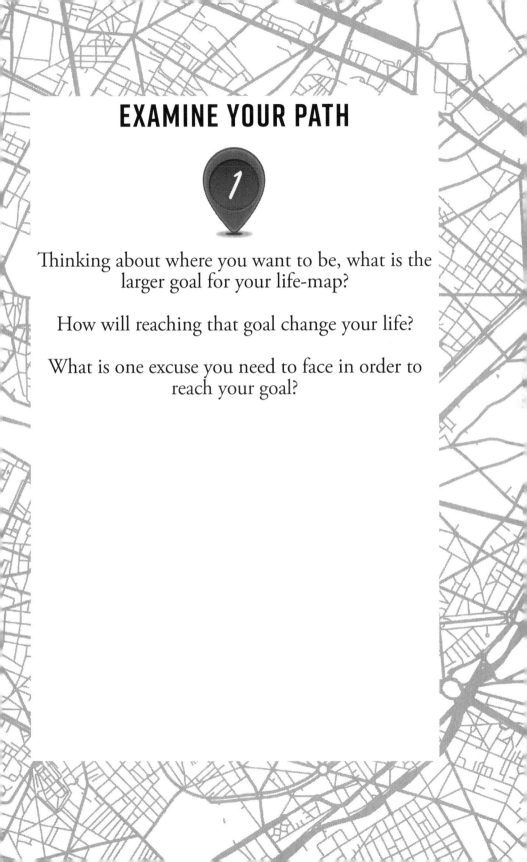

Thinking about where you want to be, what is the larger goal for your life-map?

How will reaching that goal change your life?

What is one excuse you need to face in order to reach your goal?

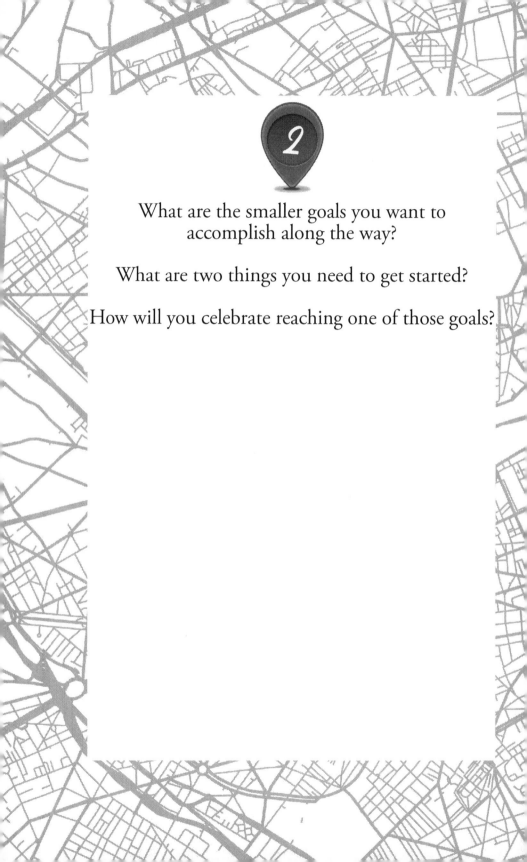

What are the smaller goals you want to
accomplish along the way?

What are two things you need to get started?

How will you celebrate reaching one of those goals?

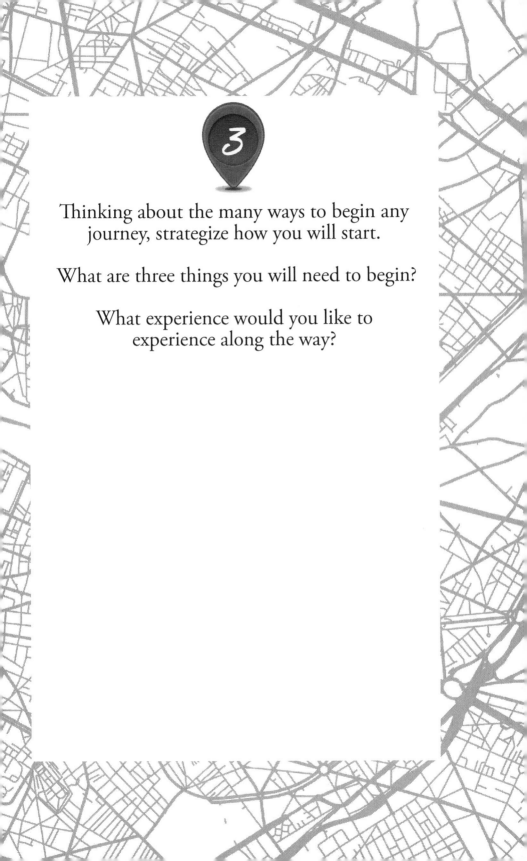

3

Thinking about the many ways to begin any
journey, strategize how you will start.

What are three things you will need to begin?

What experience would you like to
experience along the way?

EXECUTE THE ROUTE

Define your personal version of success and write it out in detail. Include the ways success would change your life.

Once you have success defined, put it somewhere you will see it daily. Commit to taking a moment every day to reflect on what you wrote down.

YOUR PERMISSION

There is no one-size-fits-all success model. Letting go of what success is supposed to look like gives us permission to own what it looks like for us.

~ LEAH MEYERS

ACCEPTING SUCCESS

Many people struggle with success because they have a preconceived idea of what it is supposed to look like and how they are supposed to get there, rather than defining what they believe success is and then figuring out how to make it happen.

There is no one-size-fits-all success model. When we let go of what we think it is supposed to look like, it gives us permission to own what success looks like for us.

The world offers so many expectations about what we should do, how we should do it, and the order we should do it in. There is a lot of great input out there, but I wanted something different. I knew for that to happen, I had to make some changes. I had to get real with myself and figure out what success meant for me. Once I made peace with what I wanted success to look like, it took the pressure off. I stopped asking for permission to live life on my own terms.

We all have an inner dialog filled with words like "but," "should," and "can't." Those mindsets will keep you stuck. For me, the shift came when I pushed past those expectations. When I did, it opened me up to new possibilities.

Every entrepreneur should know what they offer their clients. More than being an overall marketing strategy, a value proposition is a declaration of who and what you are to your customers. It tells them more than just what you offer - it tells them what you stand for, how you operate, and why they would want to do business with you. Your value proposition is about giving yourself permission to succeed.

There was a time I did not recognize or understand my own value proposition. I was following a lot of very different influencers and comparing myself to what made them successful, rather than finding my own niche. Eventually I began seeing the value I brought to the table. That shift is what allowed me to move forward and identify what success looks like for me.

If you are struggling with your value proposition, ask yourself this question: What unique value do you bring to the table?

Do not get discouraged if you cannot pinpoint it right away. Many times, the right modeling mindset comes from trial and error.

In high school I worked for a short time at a nursing home. The job was okay, but when I left, I knew without a doubt I did not want to work in the medical field. I could have skipped right past that experience, but I gave myself permission to find success in another field.

It was a valuable lesson. If we do not give ourselves permission, we will limit our potential *and* our possibilities.

GET RID OF BLACK AND WHITE THINKING

Maps commonly show roads, interstates, rivers, lakes, bridges, and landmarks in a specific area. Generally – especially when it comes to paper maps – the lay of the land is depicted in black and white. It is what it is. But the road to success is not like that. Permission to move forward in your version of success happens when you stop thinking in black and white.

When we travel, we usually stick to whatever accessible route we choose. We cannot veer off course and go through a cornfield or someone's property to get where we are going, even if that seems like the right way. Still, even with those restrictions to our route, many times, alternate routes *can* still be found or formed.

As a town develops, its road system is usually constructed to accommodate the surrounding land. For example, roads are often built around lakes or mountains. While the decisions to develop that way probably made sense to those who built the town, those black and white concepts are sometimes changed as cities expand. Roads can be rebuilt and relocated. Bridges and overpasses can be created to accommodate challenging landscapes and city infrastructure.

That is the way we move out of a black and white mindset. We look at the current lay of the land and figure out how to change, add, or work around obstacles. As you look at the impediments in your own journey, be open minded to possibility as you answer these questions:

- What is your current version of success?
- What obstacles must be dealt with?
- How would removing (or modifying) those obstacles change your journey?

Open-minded thinking gives us permission to change what needs to be changed, let go of what needs to be eliminated, and move towards whatever our version of success looks like. Facing the obstacles to success, rather than letting them define how success looks, gets us unstuck and allows us to move forward.

It is okay if you are not content with the way things are. I am not talking about being ungrateful for where you are – there is nothing worse than an attitude of entitlement. What I am encouraging you to do is give yourself permission to desire all you are capable of. Do not settle! If you do not strive to live life as the best version of you, it is likely you will end up on a hamster wheel. A life with no passion, excitement, or drive, is not a life I want to live, and I would not recommend it for anyone else either!

I have met so many people who let others decide who they are, what they can do, and who they can become. However, the most freeing thing we can do is take hold of our ability to make our own decisions. When we allow ourselves to own our independence and begin taking responsibility for the choices we make, there is a direct impact on how we view ourselves and others.

Owning your own choices shows you have respect for yourself, and often improves relationships with family, friends, and those you work with.

When I became independent for the first time. I was able to make my own decisions, and choose what I needed to move forward. I felt free for the first time. There is something very powerful about owning the choices we make. In fact, I would say, it is not possible to have true independence if we do not own our choices.

Still, we must be mindful that our choices have consequences and there is a potential impact to those closest to us. What we do – or do not do – can affect those closest to us. As I enjoyed my new freedom and independence, I was always thoughtful about the choices that had potential to impact my kids.

One shift was in the way I worked. I had always tried to work when the kids were sleeping, but I started working more when the kids were awake. It meant I was less present than I had been before, but it provided better work/life balance for me, which ultimately made life better for all of us. Before I made that change, I got real with my kids and invited them into the solution. I made sure they knew that when I spend time with them, I am one hundred percent present, and when I am busy, it is because I am working to make our future a reality. Those conversations enabled us to own the situation as a family.

I also involved them in identifying the rewards and celebrations we chose, as we worked towards our goals. We had always dreamed of owning a house and often drove through a specific neighborhood in our town, imagining ourselves living there. We used the hope of that dream to move us forward toward our home ownership goal. When you have big goals, you sometimes must make tough choices. Knowing we had the same goal, gave us permission to make decisions that may not have felt okay otherwise.

Sometimes, difficult choices must be made. In my case, any short-term choices I made were more tolerable because my kids were on the journey with me. We approached everything as a team, *together*. We planned celebrations and those drove our actions.

As I let go of preconceived notions of what success should look like, I began to make choices that worked for my children and me. Part of that change had to do with letting go of my vision of the ideal mom. I had always envisioned I would be the kind of mom who cooked every meal and had a clean house. That is just not a reality for most business owners.

Let me be clear – this one thing will shift how you see success. Let go of perfectionism! My kids can eat fast-food instead of home-cooked and that is one-hundred percent acceptable!

Besides bringing peace to our lives, this attitude has provided opportunities for my kids to be independent. Sometimes we moms work hard to build our version of perfection and it ends up robbing our kids of the opportunity to experience life. Still, there are pros and cons to this approach. When you allow your kids to become independent, you should know there are going to be times they mess up. Be okay with that because the mistakes they make are part of the learning. Let me give you an example.

My daughter plays hockey, and she had a game in a town an hour and a half away. She is responsible to grab her own equipment for games and usually does a pretty good job. But this time, right before the game, she told me she forgot her skates! I was in shock and of course went into panic mode. We could not borrow skates because she is a goalie and the ones she wears are different than the other players' skates. I thought about buying her new ones, but there were no stores nearby that sold hockey skates. Eventually, one of the hockey dads told me he had a pair of regular skates that were not sharpened. We thought it might work, since goalie skates are not sharp like regular ones. Well, thankfully they fit her, and it all worked out.

Letting my kids take responsibility meant I had to let go of control. Our lives went from me managing checklists, to having conversations as we navigated each experience and the kids managing their own checklists. The result was that we learned more about ourselves, and each other.

Know this: it is okay for life to be messy!

Just like the route you choose for any trip, there may be stops, detours, or delays. Sometimes, your route can include challenges. The process of change will not always be easy and probably will not be a straight line. My life was changing, and not only was I learning, my kids were too. The experience taught us how to make decisions that worked for us, how to pivot when challenges arose, and how to design our own journeys.

CONVERSATIONS THAT CREATE PERMISSION

Many times, the first conversation you need to have is with yourself. We can be our own worst enemies in the way we self-talk. To move past this, give yourself full permission to succeed and allow yourself room to fail.

The first step in the process is identifying what you *are* going to do and what you are *not* going to do. When we began working towards home ownership, I knew what neighborhood I wanted to live in. That neighborhood is highly desired and many times houses sell before they hit the market. We used to drive through that area and dream about what it would be like to live there. I wanted that neighborhood, but I also had to be realistic. We had to talk about it as a family and accept the reality that there was a chance it would never happen.

If I drive somewhere on my own, I take the route I want, stop when I want, and have complete control over the music.

Taking road trips with others comes with its own set of blessings and challenges. With others along, you have companionship and encouragement. However, you must also consider the needs and wants of those on the journey with you. In the same way, the people who live within the walls of your house will be affected by the decisions you make. Keep that in mind.

The most important thing you can do is let the people around you know what you are working towards. Doing that invites them to be part of the journey. When you bring others into the process, they help expand your understanding of the journey. It allows them to contribute and be a part of it; it allows you to consider things you might not otherwise consider. In today's world, the people in your home may not be your relatives. Families come in all shapes and sizes, but it does not matter. When we bring others into our journey, it stretches us and we learn to be more flexible.

When you invite others along on your journey, it is always wise to vet everyone. It is important to know who the nay-sayers and critics are and who is going to support you. Who are the cheerleaders in your circle? You will need them when you get discouraged. Who are the helpers? Ask them to help with chores or do tasks you do not need to be involved in. Let the people you trust take ownership. Allowing others to own what they are doing breeds enthusiasm. Negotiations are key, however, because it creates a home atmosphere where everyone is empowered.

YOUR TURNING POINT

Commitment requires dedication with no exceptions. This is especially true when we commit to others.

I always try to honor my commitments to others. Clearly,

there can be extenuating circumstances, but I rarely waiver from any commitment, when it is in my power to follow though. It comes down to doing what is right.

The most difficult promises to keep are those we make to ourselves. Most of us are internally wired to care what others think and to put others before ourselves; it often impacts the decision we make. Many times, if a commitment is going to be broken, it will be the one that impacts us. Still, we must honor the commitments we make to ourselves as well.

Commitments we make to ourselves open possibilities for us to receive more. It comes down to drawing a line in the sand. When you are tempted to break a commitment, ask which is more important – where you are now, or where you want to go?

Commitments make us accountable and help map our vision. Goals without commitment will remain only dreams. Commitments are what bring our vision to life and give it legs. This is where we hit "go" on GPS.

Still, know that you will not always have full control in the commitments you make. You may think you do, but sometimes there are outside influences. I had someone who provided daycare when my kids were little. They cared about my kids and did a good job, however, they were not always reliable. There were a few times I had to figure out at the last minute what I was going to do if I got to their home and no one was home. Know that you cannot control whether others keep their commitments.

Do not make your commitment so rigid you cannot adjust. When roadblocks come, you may have to change accordingly. My daycare's unreliability meant I had to pivot and make last minute arrangements so I could go to work as planned.

Be clear about your commitments. The biggest struggle many entrepreneurs have is being wishy-washy. If what you commit to is too loose, your route may become so cloudy, it opens the door to excuses. When I worked in network marketing, success relied on consultations I had with people. But what happens when potential clients keep cancelling? If you are driving and come across a roadblock, you turn around and find another route. In the same way we cannot let frustration cause us to forget our goals.

After experiencing failed relationships, my goal was to take control of my choices and build life on my terms. I decided I was not going to "need" a man. Now hear me out. This is not about pushing every man away because of a bad experience! I knew I still wanted a relationship with someone, but I did not want my happiness, success, contentment, or choices to be dependent on that. When I was young, I was dependent on others. We all are to some degree. The change for me was taking control of my own destiny and deciding what path my own life took.

Here is the upside of that work. Having boundaries drew the right people towards me and pushed away the undesirable ones. Knowing who and what I was willing to commit to, changed not only the choices I made, it changed the type of people I allowed in. Always go forward with a questioning mind. We may have opinions about what the journey should look like, but we cannot always change the road. Acceptance is part of the process, too.

Commitments are worth nothing if we do nothing with them. They should be the catalyst that drives us towards our goal. Many times, we must do something physically to solidify a commitment we make. Many successful people write out their goals. I am a visual person, so I wrote out my commitment and hung it in my office.

WRITE IT OUT

Now, it is your turn. Take a moment right now and write your commitment out. Be detailed and clear about it. Then…

- Take a picture and put it on your phone's home screen
- Hang it on your refrigerator or on your computer or laptop.
- Talk about it to those in your circle.
- Make it public.

Being clear about my own commitments helped me determine the best route to take, and kept me going when I got weary or lost focus. Because my kids were brought into the commitment, it strengthened their ownership, both on the journey there and when the goal was met.

The home we live in today was part of that journey. My kids were part of the process, so they get to be part of the goal that has been reached. It is an important life-lesson for them and has created great pride of ownership. They were able to own their own part of the journey, they picked out which room they would have, and then chose how to decorate. Part of my reward has been watching them grow and learn through my own journey.

EXAMINE YOUR PATH

Thinking about commitments you have made in the past, when have you:

Too easily given up on your commitment?

Lost site of the importance of keeping commitments?

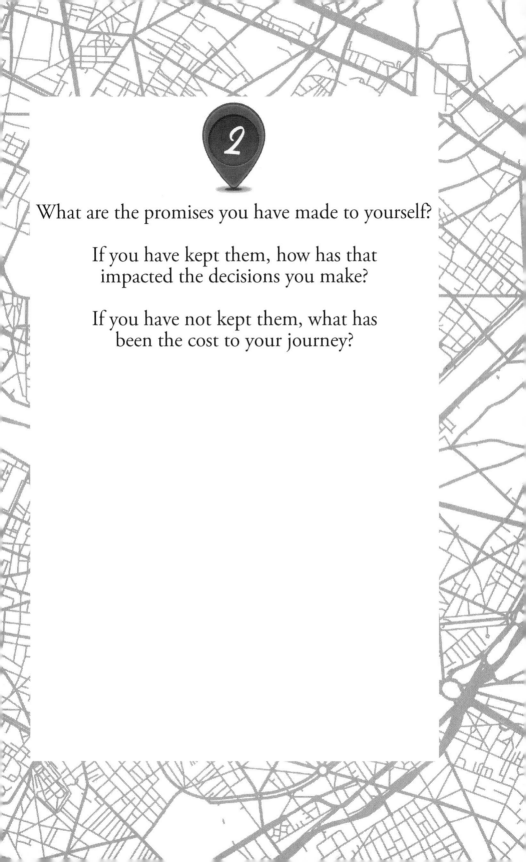

2

What are the promises you have made to yourself?

If you have kept them, how has that
impacted the decisions you make?

If you have not kept them, what has
been the cost to your journey?

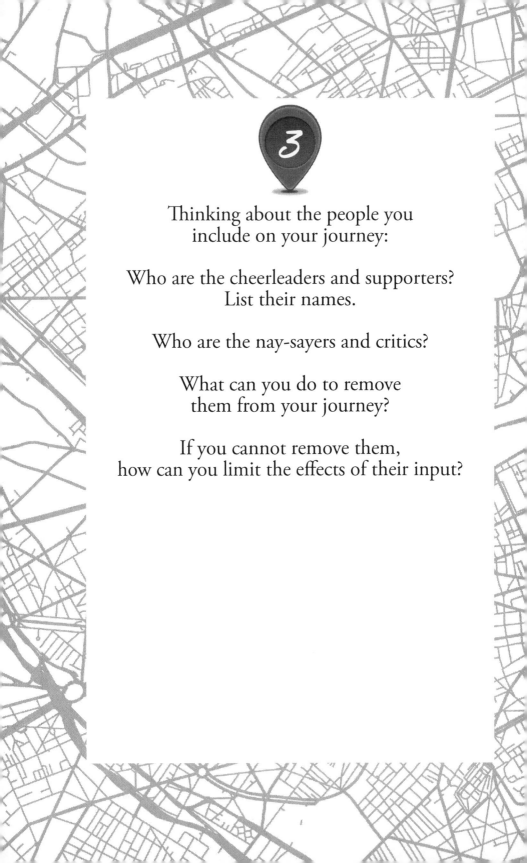

Thinking about the people you
include on your journey:

Who are the cheerleaders and supporters?
List their names.

Who are the nay-sayers and critics?

What can you do to remove
them from your journey?

If you cannot remove them,
how can you limit the effects of their input?

EXECUTE THE ROUTE

Now that you have written out and shared your
commitment statement, begin to write out
strategies for how you will stay committed to it.
Share your strategies with at least one person from
your cheerleader/supporter list.

YOUR DECISION

Success requires us to make strategic, self-accountable, and flexible decisions. Time management and planning are key to effectively managing disruptions.

~ LEAH MEYERS

KEY DECISIONS

On long road trips, we usually choose a route and then make decisions about the places we will stop, when we will gas up, and whether we will have a few rewards (like stopping for treats) along the way.

It is the same with long-term goals. Once you know the direction you are going, you must make daily decisions that keep your commitment high and move you closer to your goals. Every day we have choices and every choice we make can delay or speed up the progress of your journey. Each decision matters. You alone are responsible for the direction you take and for what you allow to impact your time and effort.

You must be strategic, self-accountable, and flexible in the decisions you make.

People are drawn to entrepreneurship for many reasons. Sometimes it is because they like the thought of not having a boss looking over them. It certainly is an advantage. However, there is good and bad to the freedom it provides. Having no boss means you get to decide what your day looks like. That is good, if you are disciplined to get to your daily goals. If you are not, it can derail your day and in the long run, potentially your business. Be realistic about what it means to be your own boss.

Another common belief is that entrepreneurs have more control of their time. That is not necessarily true. Sure, being your own boss means you have some control of when you work, and when you do not, but that is not always true. Your focus should always be on your clients, and that means there may be times you have to work more or later than you would have liked. If an emergency arises or you agree to an aggressive deadline, your work hours will likely reflect it.

Many people I have spoken to also think there is unlimited income potential. The truth is, there is no guarantee of that. When you own your own business, you must be prepared for what happens if your income changes or your business landscape changes. As I write this, we are in the middle of a pandemic. So far, it has not impacted what I am doing, but I know many entrepreneurs who have had to shift – or rethink completely – what they are doing.

Another misconception is that working for yourself is less stressful. First, there is no easy button in entrepreneurship; you get out of it what you put into it. In addition, all the pressures of business ownership are on you. For example, you are responsible for setting up health insurance, managing investments, tracking (and potentially paying) taxes, and if you have employees, you will do all that for them as well.

There are many influencers out there who will tell you the great advantages of being an entrepreneur and there are many rewards. However, I want you to go into this with your eyes wide open and your mind prepared for the realities of owning a business. Self-accountability is key. Know yourself, know your weaknesses, and expect that the journey will include unknowns, delays, and challenges.

When you determine your day-to-day goals, recognize that circumstances outside your control may impact how efficiently the day goes. To stay on track daily, I identify key decisions I need to make and figure out how I am going to stay focused and committed to them. It is somewhat like using GPS to plan your route. You plug in the destination then pick the route that best fits the need for that day. Still, nothing is perfect and sometimes flexibility is needed. Avoid becoming fixed on a specific route to your daily goal and give yourself room for detours and delays.

When your journey includes others, your carefully created schedule can be impacted by their needs. Since I have kids, I am constantly scheduling appointments such as lessons, friend visits, or dentist appointments. I make every attempt to be efficient and usually build buffer time into the calendar. Most of the time that works well, but not always. Recently I took my kids to a dentist appointment and thought I had fleshed out the time to get there, the time for the appointment, and the trip home. Well, even my careful calculating did not account for the dentist running behind.

Many things can shift or change your schedule. I live in rural Minnesota where there is often roadwork or farm equipment blocking or delaying my route. We have extreme weather that can impact travel and cause dangerous driving conditions. Ignoring the weather could cause you to end up stuck in a ditch or have unplanned overnight stays. And, if that were not enough, during harvest months, we need to be aware of deer on roads. If I was set on one way to travel, I might allow roadblocks, detours, snow, or deer to determine the destination. Instead, I have learned to adjust and pivot. I take alternate routes when machinery or roadwork blocks the way, avoid driving when the weather is dangerous, and travel in daylight hours during harvest.

This is where time management often comes into play. Many people assume entrepreneurship equates with unlimited free time and you may find unexpected interruptions come when others believe that working from home means you are available. Time management and planning are going to be key to your ability to manage disruptions.

You must know how to manage time and be accountable because delays can accumulate and impact your productivity. Set appropriate boundaries to control unexpected time grabbers before they add up.

If your route changes, do not panic; adjust. Being dead-set on going ahead no matter the situation can derail you in life changing ways. Adjust according to the conditions.

Everyone has things that distract them, or cause them to lose focus. I call those things shiny objects or "Look-there's-a-squirrel" moments. For some, it comes in the form of procrastination; why do today, what you can put off until tomorrow, or better yet, next week. There is only one way to deal with procrastination – you just have to discipline yourself. Remind yourself that when the work is done, you have time to relax or celebrate.

Another struggle many people have is unexpected distractions. The truth is, interruptions are guaranteed in life; the trick is to avoid letting them sidetrack you. One thing I do to handle the distractions is to keep notes on my desk, so if the distraction is a thought or a to-do, I can write it down so it does not take up my brain power at that moment. Disrupting the shiny object can keep you on track.

When tempted by shiny objects, I ask myself what the urgency is. If it is something pressing – such as sick children or urgent client issues – it is non-negotiable. Go do what you must.

If what is distracting you is not urgent, ask yourself if it is the appropriate time to yield to the interruption. If the time works, fine. If not, figure out if it can be scheduled for a better time. I often schedule my distraction. During the holidays, I am a sucker for Hallmark movies and I used to get distracted when I knew they were on. Now, I try to schedule watch-time. It gives me time for what otherwise would become a distraction. I also make sure the time I put towards it is not excessive. That means no binge-watching one after another!

There are pros and cons of every choice we make and every choice has consequences. When friends ask me to go to lunch, it may mean I need to work later that night. In the end, I allow myself the opportunity to take advantage of those distractions, if the cost is something I can accept. Sometimes it is okay to add time for things that give you joy.

The biggest decision we make as entrepreneurs is around our ethics. What are the moral principles that define your business? Integrity sits deep within us and you alone decide how it influences your choices. For me, it comes down to the influence I have on my children and the legacy I want to leave. I want my kids to see me doing what I am supposed to do. No one is watching you, but it still matters. I do the same thing every day – whether someone is watching or not!

LIFE CHANGING DECISIONS

There was a time when I was stuck. I believed there had to be more to life than living paycheck to paycheck and constantly having to check my bank account to see if I could afford something the kids needed. I was sick of living that way, and it was clear that something had to change, but I was not sure how to make that happen. Then, as I searched for a way to change my circumstances, a friend told me about Upwork. It is a company that connects businesses with freelancers to fill the gap for short-term tasks, full-time contract work, or recurring projects. I thought it might be a stepping stone where I could make some money, explore my degree, and catch my breath after the previous few years of change. It was the blessing I needed.

When my first Upwork contract began, it provided enough for my short-term financial goals. That eliminated any fear I had about my ability to make it work. I was still a bit skeptical, but I made it my goal to apply for at least six jobs a day.

What I did not realize was how much Upwork would change my life.

EXAMINE YOUR PATH

How will you pivot when unexpected interruptions shift or change your schedule?

What is one shiny object you could schedule?

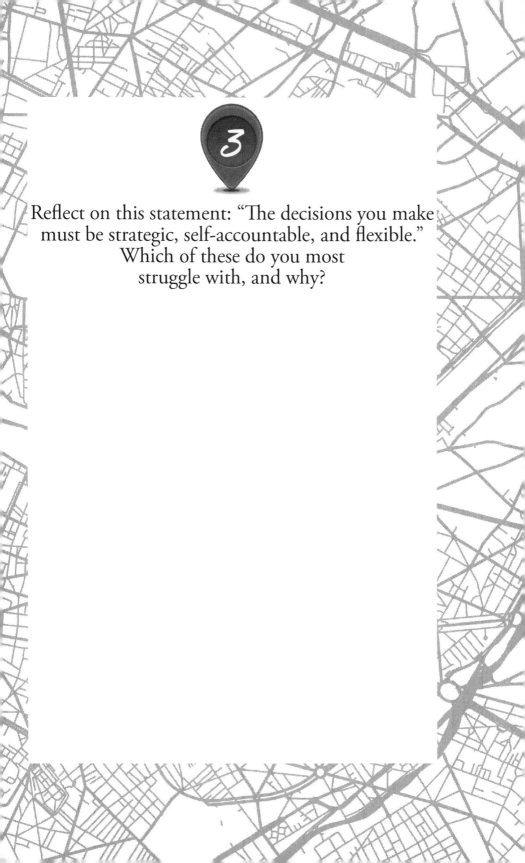

Reflect on this statement: "The decisions you make must be strategic, self-accountable, and flexible." Which of these do you most struggle with, and why?

EXECUTE THE ROUTE

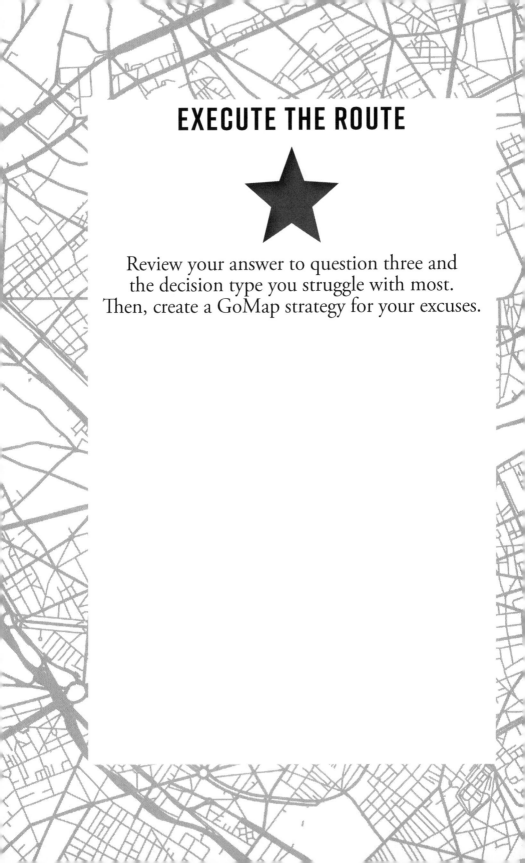

Review your answer to question three and
the decision type you struggle with most.
Then, create a GoMap strategy for your excuses.

Part 2

GROWING

YOUR LAUNCH

*Courage is not the lack of fear; it is moving through
fear towards your goal, despite what you feel.*

~ LEAH MEYERS

When I first moved to Northern Minnesota, I had applied for local jobs but was not getting called for interviews. The one interview I *did* have was for an assisted living facility, but I was not hired because I was *too* innovative and had too many new ideas. I was frustrated, but I needed to work, so Upwork became a more viable option.

I had been an entrepreneur, most of my adult life, so when the idea of Upwork came along, I was interested but hesitant at the same time. It was quite different from anything I had done before, but I saw the possibilities and potential. Upwork offered a lot of freedom, but at that time, it seemed to me there was a potential to have multiple bosses, which could be tricky to navigate. I committed to giving it a go for at least six months, and dug in and started applying for jobs. By the time I was six months in, I was at my max capacity for clients I could take on.

The jobs I found allowed me to make a living, but I wanted more. We lived in a wealthy community and that brings its own financial challenges. My kids were growing and of course their needs grew too. I wanted to provide for them, so I began forming a strategy to launch my career in a more planned out way.

Early on, with Upwork, I committed to applying for a minimum of five jobs every day. It was a great approach, but at the end of the first thirty days, the types of jobs I was hired for ended up being oddly random, which made the experience a bit chaotic. I changed that by dividing job postings into these categories.

- ✓ Jobs I can do.
- ✓ Jobs I would like to do.
- ✓ Jobs I would love to do.
- ✓ Jobs I would never do.

By determining which jobs best aligned with my goals, I was not only saving time and energy, I was increasing my potential opportunity. Eliminating jobs that I would never do may seem like a no-brainer, but it allowed me to concentrate my energy towards the ones that could propel me forward. With my search narrowed down, I consistently and purposefully applied for the jobs I was most interested in and most qualified for.

When your chosen path is not working for you, or the road is full of potholes, look at your original destination and adjust the route accordingly. My goal was never to make Upwork my sole income. It was intended to be a stepping stone, or a short detour, so I could regroup and figure out where I wanted to go. Clearly it was time to pivot again.

I decided on a more focused approach. I began to apply only for jobs that used Kajabi, which is an all-in-one, online learning platform. I focused on strategy and development for course creators and entrepreneurs looking to build memberships. I filled any skill gaps by learning everything I could about the platform and taking as many courses I could find in course creation and membership development. I was going to become an expert!

Narrowing down the types of jobs I applied for was not my only strategy. Here are a few other things I did:

- As lower paying clients left, I looked for higher paying clients, which was a straightforward way to increase financially.
- I aligned with influencers. If you want to go higher, get to know others who are successful.
- I searched out opportunities to increase my value proposition. Being the go-to person in your field increases opportunity and drives success.
- As my experience and reputation grew, I began applying for higher paying jobs. Your pay should match your experience level.

With these strategies in place, I began to make traction towards my goal.

The most important thing you can do as an entrepreneur is to work with integrity. My goal was to provide above-par work, while focusing on customer service. I poured everything into my clients, which made me an asset to them. Loyal customers are the mainstay of any business because repeat business creates profitable relationships and stability.

GET IT DONE

Any long trip takes mental strength. It is easy to lose focus or become distracted on very extended journeys. In the same way, when we launch a business or set out on a goal campaign, there is a potential for our mindset to derail us. When you are working on long term goals, attitude is *everything*!

One of the chief obstacles we face is our inability to allow imperfection. This may seem like a radical thing to say, but it is more important to get something done than it is to be perfect. I am not saying it is okay to do *anything* halfway. As I have said before, integrity is important. We should always do our best and give our all to what we do. What I am saying is that we can get stuck in a never-ending cycle of trying to make something perfect. It is like being stuck in one of those roundabouts. You drive around the circle over and over, but never get to the actual destination intended. Enough said!

One-way thinking can also sidetrack us. Sometimes we get stuck because we only allow ourselves to see one way of doing something. If you are on a road that only goes north, but your goal is to go west, you are going to have to change direction. There are usually several ways to do that, so allow yourself to test different options while you figure out what works best.

Another place people get stuck is thinking their journey should look like someone else's. We do ourselves a great disservice when we try to copy others. Most of the successful entrepreneurs I know are authentic to who they are and do not mind being different. Whatever you do, give yourself permission to put your own spin on what your experience will look like.

Finally, be okay with failure. Like every long-term journey, detours often provide learning opportunities. You cannot predict where every road will lead, but you can learn from every situation. My third job through Upwork was as a project manager. It seemed like something I might enjoy; however, it did not take me long to figure out that was not where I wanted to be. I pushed ahead, made it work, and completed the project, but I learned a big lesson – I do not like project management work. It is okay if you go down the wrong road. If you do, just recalculate and get going again.

Stop letting your feelings get in the way of your goal. If you do everything you can to be successful, you can be confident about who you are and what you do. Use strategy and knowledge to drive the work you do and stay authentic and honest. Say what you will do and do what you say. At the end of the day, satisfaction is about knowing you did your best for your clients. It cannot be about dollar signs.

ROADBLOCKS TO YOUR GOAL

It is human nature to make excuses. However, excuses are the main reason many people do not reach their goals. Moving past the justifications we make takes strategy and that means looking at them head on.

I love this quote by Brendon Burchard: "Who needs your A-Game Today?"

It is my go-to on those days when I am just not feeling it. Yes, I have those days! Everyone does. When I do, I remind myself that my clients expect me to bring my A-game. If you are facing a day like that, I recommend you do this:

- Recognize it for what it is – a moment. One off day does not mean you have failed.

- Face it. Do not try to ignore it and power through. That approach can lead to guilt, which is a fast-track to doubt.
- Do not let it get you stuck. Here is how:
    - Take a short break and allow yourself a moment. For example, spend thirty minutes journaling all the reasons you do not feel like working. At the end of the thirty minutes, set the journal aside and go back to work.
    - Set up an immediate quick reward. For example, get your work done and reward yourself by going shopping, getting a massage, or going to the gym.

When I am in the middle of an off day, I remind myself that I also need my A-game. For me, it is about integrity. I am always conscious of the fact that my goal is to always do my best for my client. Honor is a great motivator for me.

A great strategy to help me avoid off-days is not scheduling work on the weekends. There was a time when work bled into the weekends. When I allowed that to happen, I had more days during the week where I felt burned out. Being strategic about work/life balance is an important way to mitigate off days.

COST

I talk to people all the time who want to launch businesses. People have many reasons why they do not think their idea will work, but one of the most common objections I hear is the financial cost. Here are just a few of the reasons I hear. Check mark the ones you have said or thought:

- "I don't have that kind of money."
- "I have to save for a while."
- "I could never afford that."
- "I cannot imagine making that kind of money."
- "I don't need much to live on."
- "I don't want to have to pay taxes on that much money."
- "First I need to pay for [fill in your excuse]."
- "I'll do it after [fill in your excuse]."

When someone tells me lack of money is the problem, I suggest they identify the value of their investment. Understanding your return on investment will help you prepare how you can overcome the obstacle of money. Here are a few strategies to build cash:

- Build sweat equity by doing your own work. For example, you could create your own content, or website.
- Trade work with other entrepreneurs. For example, if you can write, trade services with someone who does social media management or builds websites.
- Identify ways to build capital. For example, you could cash in stocks, pull from investment accounts or sell unwanted items.
- Determine ways to control output. For example, you could reduce unnecessary expenses or pare down entertainment expenses for a time.

In the end, it is up to you. I have always found that we invest in what we value the most. Figure out how much you want this and then determine how to make it work.

What many people fail to consider is the true price of doing business. There is always a cost to lifestyle and time. Running a business can impact us physically, emotionally, and/or spiritually. There will be a cost of time and commitment. Here are just a few of the reasons people give. Check mark the ones you have said or thought:

- "I already don't have enough time."
- "When will I have time to do that?"
- "I have no idea how that would work."
- "I do not have a support system."
- "I'll have to find someone to do that for me."
- "I don't want to have to give that up."
- "I have to do that myself because no one else can."
- "This won't work, it's not the right way."
- "I like things done my own way."
- "I have really high standards."
- "I don't like to give up my free time."

Know that when you launch a business, your life will be impacted in ways you may not be able to predict. Identify how you will approach the non-money related impacts to owning a business. Here are a few strategies you can put in place:

- Evaluate what you will and will not do.
- Decide which areas you can give up control.
- Identify where you can divide your time.
- Build a circle of people you can trust and rely on.
- Determine what tasks, chores, or work you can hand off and to whom.
- Evaluate all the roles you have and how you can adjust.

- Identify your weak areas and figure out how you can compensate for those areas.

FEARS

Fear can be a powerful force that keeps us from reaching our goals. It usually comes from an internal place, often because of past experiences, but can develop because of a lack of experience or self-confidence. Here are just a few fears I have heard people share. Check mark the ones you have said or thought:

- "What will happen if…."
- "If this happens, then…."
- "How will I cope if…"
- "I won't be okay if [insert situation here] happens."

We often get in our own way by over thinking, second-guessing, or over-analyzing. Courage is not the lack of fear; it is moving through the fear you have and moving towards your goal despite what your feelings are telling you. When fear strikes, here are a few strategies you can put in place:

- Determine that the "what if" is not as great as what you want to accomplish.
- Create a list of times your fears never happened.
- Resolve that there is little chance that what you fear would happen.
- Write down statements that are the opposite of your fear. For example: Snakes are more afraid of me than I am of them.

BAD MINDSETS

Thoughts are one of the most powerful influences in our lives. What we think can influence the choices we make, which can determine our success or failure. The right mindset can influence our happiness, hope, opportunities, and successes. Facing thoughts that could hold you back is a strategy you cannot afford to skip. Here are just a few bad mindsets. Check mark the ones you have said or thought:

- "I'm not sure I can do that."
- "I'm not qualified for this."
- "If people really knew me, they'd know I can't do this."
- "I'm not strong (capable, smart, clever, etc.) enough."
- "No one will hire me, because…"
- "I've never done this before."
- "This is too complicated."
- "I'm too lazy to do this."
- "There's no way it will work."
- "The change is too big."
- [Write your negative thoughts here]

This is one of the hardest things to push past. However, when stinking thinking is not dealt with, its effects can be seen in everything we do. Self-talk is critical; if you think you cannot do it, you will not do it! When you are stuck because of your thought-life, shift your mindset with these strategies:

- Decide it is an opportunity to learn something new.
- If something has you stumped, tackle it from a different angle.

- Identify other ways to make it work.
- Write down three strengths that qualify you to meet your goal.
- Ask one of your cheerleaders why they think you *can* meet your goal.
- Name another time you accomplished something you set out to do.

SELF CONFIDENCE

Self-talk is critical and lack of confidence is the number one thing that stops people from reaching their goals. If you came here doubting your confidence, let me encourage you. By reading this far into this book, you have already shown courage and confidence. Stop saying you have no self-assurance; just agree that you have it.

Be confident in who you are, even when others are not! Remember when I told you about my job interview? I was rejected because of my strengths. At that moment in time, I did not feel confident or comfortable in my skin. But I *did* know who I was. That rejection caused something in me to rise.

I was told I was too forward thinking and had too many ideas. I realized right then, I had to own what I did with that information. I am an innovator and a visionary. Instead of seeing denial as a bad thing, I used the words to lift me up and push me forward. It ended up being a good thing because had I gotten the job, I probably would not be where I am today.

The message is clear. Do not stop just because someone does not appreciate your abilities. The qualities that make you successful will not always be sought out by others. When you experience rejection, decide how you will respond. Take time to reorient and use that time to take some risks.

Times like this can be a great opportunity to do something that might not feel so safe. Stretching yourself can be exhilarating and you may learn things about yourself that surprise you!

Years ago, a friend asked me to take a road trip on a motorcycle. We had no plan; the intent was to just see where the road would take us. If you knew me, you would know how out of character that was. NO plan? On a motorcycle with no protection? Limiting what I might need to what will fit a tiny bag? It seemed insane. Still, I pushed myself out of my comfort zone. We ended up in St. Louis, Missouri, then Indianapolis, Indiana, where we decided to head to Nashville, Tennessee. In the end we traveled thirty-five hundred miles in six days. I was stretched, but I saw and experienced new and wonderful things I would have missed if I had not jumped all in.

This quote says it all:

"You have to learn to get comfortable being uncomfortable. You have to be willing to get out of your comfort zone and push your limits." ~Jesse Itzler

My encouragement to you is to let yourself be open to change. Try new things and get outside your comfort zone. Unexpected is not always bad, and sometimes change leads to happy surprises.

EXAMINE YOUR PATH

How has a need for perfection stopped you from reaching your goal?

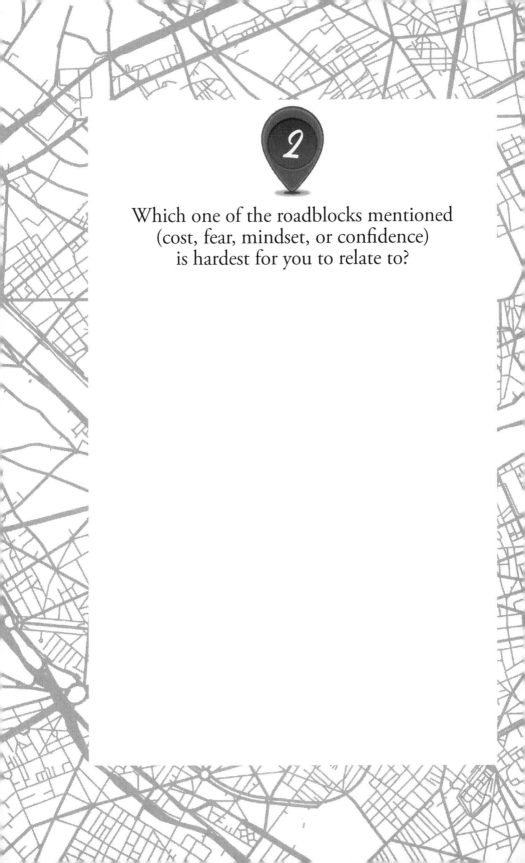

Which one of the roadblocks mentioned
(cost, fear, mindset, or confidence)
is hardest for you to relate to?

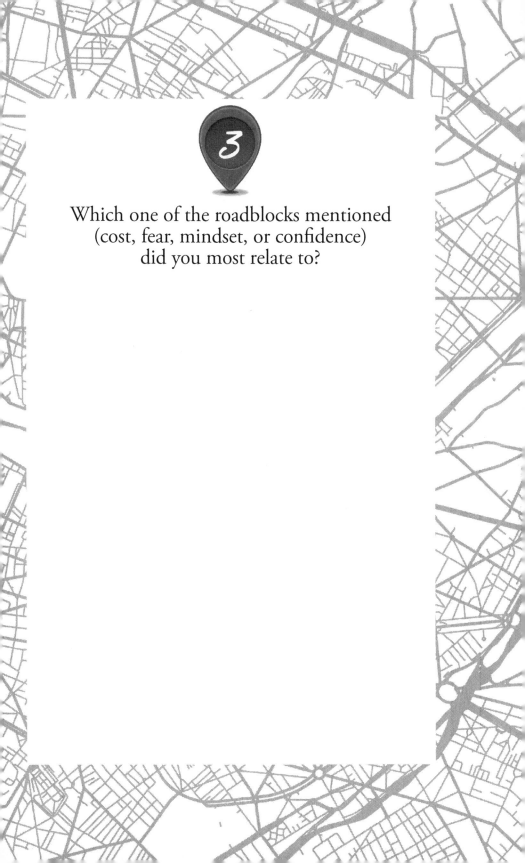

Which one of the roadblocks mentioned
(cost, fear, mindset, or confidence)
did you most relate to?

EXECUTE THE ROUTE

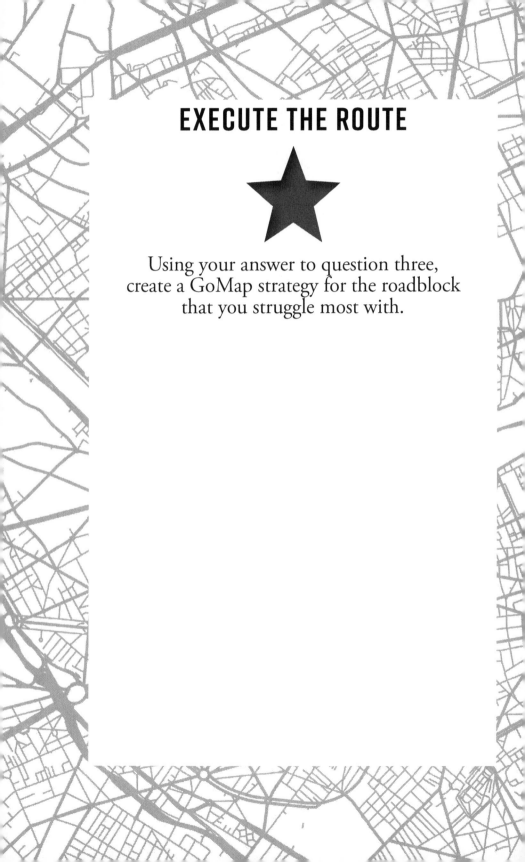

Using your answer to question three,
create a GoMap strategy for the roadblock
that you struggle most with.

YOUR LIFESTYLE

Every successful entrepreneur must examine what they will,
or will not, allow. Doing that ensures there is always
enough left for what is important to you.

~ LEAH MEYERS

WORKAHOLIC MODE

As I focused on my goals and vision, my business grew. Great
things were happening and there was a shift in our lifestyle. I still
worked hard, but my kids and I were also enjoying life.

It was always my vision to provide my kids with choices and
a big one I wanted to give them was a Christmas experience.
When I became financially independent, I gave my kids the option to choose presents or a vacation experience. I was happy
when they chose the latter. They both decided Las Vegas would
be their experience. We had been there before, but always on a
budget. This time was different. In the past, we were limited to
doing what we could afford, but this trip we did whatever we

wanted!

We ate wherever the kids wanted to go, saw a show every day, and a highlight was going to a Vegas Golden Knights hockey game. It was a reward for hard work and I was thrilled that I could provide them with an experience like that.

There were practical considerations, too. My kids were growing up and every parent knows that as kids grow up, it usually means additional expenses for things like hobbies and sports. As they got bigger, so did their needs, and the cost to provide those needs. Still, like most parents, I wanted to provide well for them, so I did not mind working harder to make sure they were cared for.

My belief in myself was different, too. I worked at full capacity and truly believed in myself. Negative mindsets like imposter syndrome and fear were gone. As my confidence grew, people noticed, and started to seek me out consistently.

The success made me wonder how far I could take my business. All along, I had been challenging myself with step goals. But now, every time I met one, all I could think about was what I could do next. I was still working towards my main goal, but the step goals became more about topping what I had just completed. Eventually, my monthly earnings became the driving force of the goals I set. For example, one week I decided to see what would happen if I worked one hundred hours. I did it, and it was crazy, but it also made me want to push even further.

There is nothing wrong with setting goals that lead to success, but if we set goals without considering the cost, it can come back to bite us.

Around this time, I noticed my kids were spending more time on their phones and technology devices. I had been so busy; I had missed it. My busyness had allowed the nonstop technology to creep in. This was the beginning of the pandemic. We were all home, they were working on school, and had a lot more free time. My workload was a lot because I didn't know what the next month would bring. I was working as much as I could, knowing that I could be out of work.

I knew things had to change. I had to do *something*; the kids needed me, my time, and my focus on them. I let them know that when school started, their technology was going to be limited. As I worked with the kids to limit technology and look for other things to do, I began to see some shocking parallels in me. Sometimes, we must take a good look at ourselves to identify what is at the heart of a situation. After some self-reflection, it was clear I had become addicted to work. I was a workaholic.

A workaholic is someone who works excessively and has difficulty detaching from work regardless of the impact to their physical health, mental state, or to relationships. Like any addict, there is a draw for the workaholic. It may be a financial reward, recognition, or success, but since the perceived reward(s) are more socially acceptable, the addiction may go on for some time unnoticed. Like many other addictions, it can sneak up on the person.

Once I became aware of the impact of my own workaholism, I knew I had to act. I started by looking at what had driven my addiction. Clearly, I am self-motivated and like to push myself, which is good; those traits are important if you want to be a successful entrepreneur. However, it is vital to use moderation to balance out motivations. Looking back, I see that my constant need to meet higher and higher goals became its own kind of hamster wheel. For me, working was a way to escape, and to keep from thinking about things. When I was working, I could block out the world and numb any feelings I was not comfortable with.

Unlike other addictions, no one questioned my behavior, because work is what we do. However, I eventually had to face it head on. My kids are my *why* and seeing how it impacted them was enough reason to change my behavior. Like every other shift in my life, I developed strategies to help me modify my approach to work.

BUDGET YOUR TIME

Many times, people get into trouble financially when they spend more than they have. We can do that with time, too. Just like money, we can also waste time or spend it unwisely. Most of us are familiar with financial budgets – at least on some level. Budgets help us use money in more purposeful ways. I took the same approach to shift my time priorities and create a better work/life balance.

Time is an investment, so make sure you are doing what you need to do.

The first step is to take inventory of where your time is spent. You will need that in order to prioritize what needs your attention and time. Here is an example of my time inventory:

1. My kids and family. They are my number one priority, so the time they need from me is high priority.
2. My faith. Faith is a big part of my life, so time for devotions, Bible study, and Church must be factored in.
3. My clients. It is my goal to give my clients my best, so time dedicated to serving them plays an important role

in my time budget. I include time to do work *and* to care for one-off needs or concerns that come up.

Do not forget to factor in everyday tasks such as cooking, driving, laundry, and cleaning. If you do not include those, you will find they creep in anyway, and disrupt your time budget. I have also started adding other things such as self-care time, fun, and date nights. Work time can easily push these out if you are not purposeful about scheduling them.

I recommend you live with your time-budget for a period, and then reexamine it. As you look at what worked and what did not, identify where there are gaps, what you may have missed, and where you are doing too much or too little. This will help you find the time budget that works best for you, your work, and those in your home.

As you act on your strategy, know these types of changes do not happen overnight. Give yourself grace. The key is to start somewhere, be purposeful about your plan, and keep going until it works for you.

SAYING NO

The two biggest changes I made were learning to say *no*, and setting proper boundaries.

For some, saying *no* is difficult. We often avoid it because we do not like conflict or think others will see us in a negative way. But learning to say *no* is part of life, and certainly part of doing business, because it shows that we value ourselves and our time.

Since my kids have played hockey for several years, it is a big part of our lives, and we are passionate about the sport. There was a time when I was asked to join the hockey board. I was very tempted. It seemed like a natural progression and I could see how great it would be to be supportive in a more substantial way. However, I also knew the cost it would have on my family and business. As much as I would have liked to take the position, I said *no* because I knew the cost was greater than the benefit.

There are many reasons we struggle to say *no*, even though we know something is the right decision. For one, being asked feels good. It is a compliment when we are chosen and saying *no* can feel like shutting down praise. Maybe it feels like you can make a difference and saying *no* feels like defeat. Sometimes it feels as though saying *no* is in some way offending the person who asked.

Taking our emotions out of the equation can make it easier to clearly decline something that is not right for us. Making the decision from a practical strategy takes some of the fear away. Here are some ways to know you should say *no*.

Say no if:
- It would have a negative impact on the priorities you have committed to. Robbing Peter to pay Paul never works out well in the long term.
- It does not align with your goals or vision – especially if it takes you further away from them.
- It does not align with your ethics or compromises your integrity.
- You would be doing it for the wrong motive such as affirmation, recognition, or because of another's opinion.
- The long-term gain is not worth short-term sacrifice.

SETTING BOUNDARIES

Without boundaries or limits, there is no way to identify if our needs and expectations are correctly aligned with our priorities. As entrepreneurs, we alone set up boundaries because we alone understand the long-term impact to our time and business.

Boundaries should clearly convey what your clients can expect from you. They should also communicate your business needs and strategies to family and friends. Every successful entrepreneur must examine what they will, or will not allow. Even people who have successfully navigated personal boundaries, often must work through boundaries in their business.

One of the biggest complaints I hear from other entrepreneurs is the disregard for work time – especially when working from home. One way to avoid the interruptions that come with that mindset is to make it clear that when you are working, you are working. It is about being clear about the expectation. Setting parameters around your time allows you to be focused and attentive to clients and your work. Intentionality breeds productivity and allows you to enjoy nonwork time more.

However, you should know that even well stated boundaries will be tested. Life has a way of interrupting even the best-defined plan. Find a way to make work boundaries make sense for your situation. For example, my kids school district has experienced distance learning over the last year, which means they attend school online, from home. They are old enough to fend for themselves for the most part. Still, there are times they want and need my attention. I want to be there for them when necessary. So, when they are attending school from home, I use that time to make calls. When they are not at home, I work on projects, which allows me to work uninterrupted.

Your workload should fit the season of life you are in. I would have never been able to work to the capacity I currently work now when my kids were small. If I had toddlers at home, my work time would be based on what worked best for their schedule. For example, I might work when they nap or after they go to bed at night. If you have littles, give yourself permission to be in the moment with them. Life is too short to miss those seasons with your children.

If you have no children at home, boundaries are still important – especially if your home is shared with others. Make sure you are clear on what you need and do not shy away from boundaries because of guilt or other's expectations. Your situation is unique and your circumstances should determine your boundaries.

Like everything else, time and boundaries are subject to change. If I am on the road and find myself delayed because of traffic or a train crossing, I have no choice but to adjust. The purpose of budgeting time and learning to say no is not to eliminate all interruptions, delays, or changes to our plan. Clearly setting boundaries is a strategy that, when done well, helps us navigate the sometimes-changing route that is work/life balance.

EXAMINE YOUR PATH

How have you used work to avoid dealing with unpleasant or uncomfortable situations? Name two ways being a workaholic has impacted your life.

2

What are two or three ways you
"over spend" your time?

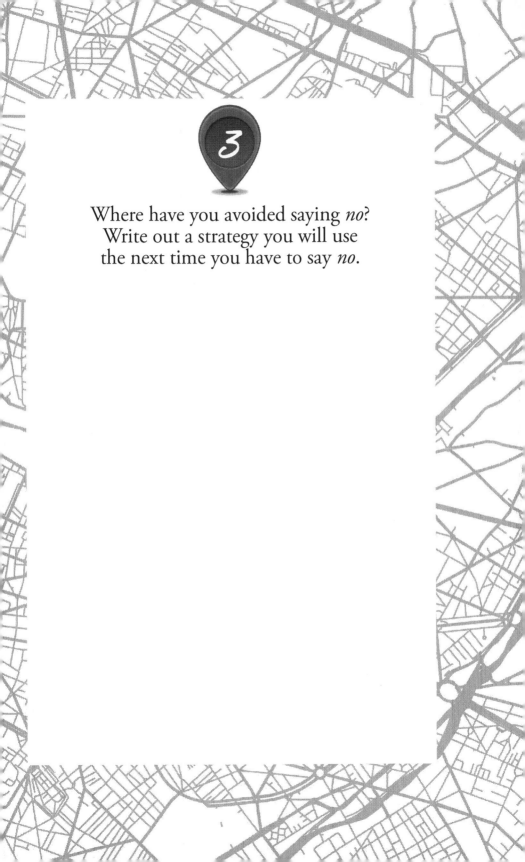

3

Where have you avoided saying *no*?
Write out a strategy you will use
the next time you have to say *no*.

4

Where is one place you need to set boundaries?

How can you set an appropriate boundary for that situation?

Who should be made aware of that boundary?

EXECUTE THE ROUTE

The first step in better time budgeting is to take inventory of where your time is spent. Make a list of your top 4 priorities. Then, prioritize them to indicate which ones most need your attention and time.

YOUR GROWTH

Vision puts your focus on the destination, not the twists and turns
in the road. You alone choose how much and how hard to push.

~ LEAH MEYERS

VISUALIZE YOUR DESTINATION

When you set out on a long trip, it is important to have a clear
understanding of what it will take to get you there. Long journeys can include detours, delays, and unexpected challenges. If
you have ever been in a car for extended periods, you know the
endurance that is required. Keeping your eyes on the destination
is key when you travel – especially on very long trips.

In the same way, focusing on your long-term vision is a necessary part of every business and personal journey. Casting my
vision kept me on track with my bigger goal of financial freedom
when the way there seemed frustrating or daunting. I knew what
my overall vision was and home ownership was a big part of that

goal, so I was willing to do what it takes to make that a reality.

House hunting can be exciting and challenging, but looking for a home in the middle of a pandemic was a whole other experience! In our state, things were shut down, but we began driving around to look at houses. At first it was just a way to get out of the house and do a bit of dreaming. Then a house in my ideal neighborhood came on the market. I knew I had to at least look at it.

Since we were in a pandemic and housing was a hot market, some realtors wouldn't put an offer in unless you had a pre-approval letter. I found a realtor willing to show me the home that was on the market in the neighborhood I had been driving through for a long time. The showing was at nine o'clock in the morning and as soon as I saw it, I knew I wanted it. As exciting as that was, there was still a question of financing.

I still needed a pre-approval letter to increase the chance my offer would be accepted. It was going to be tricky to find a mortgage lender who would work with me; an entrepreneur in the middle of a pandemic. In just two years, my salary had increased just over six times and the banks I talked to in the past were having a difficult time reconciling how I could have done that. As banks refused to finance me, I knew I had to do something because without financing, my offer would be rescinded.

There was a time I would have accepted *no* as the final answer, but not now. There had to be a way to make this work! I knew of a non-local mortgage broker who could potentially help. Her information had been hanging on my refrigerator for months, so I raced home and called. I explained what was going on and by five o'clock that night I had a pre-approval letter.

Pre-approval was only the first hurdle, though. In order to buy the house, I needed a specific dollar amount to close and it was a very large number and more than I had readily available. It seemed like an impossible hurdle, but I made an offer anyway.

Houses in that area were selling within hours, but our offer was submitted. By the end of the day, there were several offers. Again, it seemed like it might not happen. But rather than give up, I asked the real estate agent to include a statement to the owners about my desire to live in the neighborhood. The telephone call that day is etched in my mind. When I answered, the real estate agent said, "Well…." and then paused. I prepared myself for the worst, but in the next breath he told me my offer was accepted. I was on my way to home ownership. It was surreal!

Still, the reality was, I had two months to have a very large down payment. I knew I could do it. Every step goal I had set and reached was practice for this moment. I hung up the phone, walked into the house, and set a plan in motion. I involved the kids in the discussion. The goal meant, I would be working a lot, so we all had to pitch in. At the end of the conversation, we each understood what was needed for this to work.

As exciting as that first night was, reality eventually sunk in. The next few weeks were going to be daunting, but we stayed focused on our goal and faced any challenges head-on.

In the best circumstances, the mortgage process can be unnerving. The underwriting, appraisal, and loan approval process can be tricky and complex to navigate. Completing the process during a pandemic had its own set of challenges. Two weeks before closing, our loan was still in underwriting. It could have stopped us, but we were able to get through that hurdle and closed in July this year.

It was not a straightforward, or simple process, and many times I could have lost hope. There were several times I had to fight the voices that tried to say I did not deserve it or I could not do it. We can be our own worst enemies when it comes to meeting challenging or difficult goals. Do not let yourself get into a bad mindset. Fight the urge to give up by reminding yourself why you are on this journey. Concentrating on the goal can change the voices that say you cannot do it.

Keep your eyes on the bigger goal. Vision matters because it keeps you focused on the destination, not the twists and turns in the road.

BUCKETS OF MONEY

When it comes to managing money, many people struggle to save for big goals. Becoming financially independent and purchasing a house began with a plan. Early on, my budget was more about paying for necessities than big purchases. When I made my first thousand dollars on Upwork, I was happy to have enough to make ends meet. Eventually, as my income increased, I paid off debt, and created a savings plan for future purchases.

The system I developed helped me manage my finances in a way that worked for me. What I did was funnel money into buckets allocated for specific goals and purposes such as necessities, obligations, and wants. It was a straightforward way to meet current and future financial needs.

When I started working, money was sometimes tight; it was mostly about making enough for necessities. As my income increased and I began to have disposable income, it became even more important to be clear about where my money was spent.

Many people over spend and get into trouble as they begin to make more money because they do not plan for success. When money comes in, they begin spending it on everything they ever wanted. We have all heard the stories of people who win the lottery and within a short time have nothing. It is critical to figure out your financial strategy before you reach a level of success.

Sometimes, people struggle to understand the difference between a need and a want. For example, needs include things like a place to live, clothing to wear, and food and water. Wants are those "nice to have" things, like eating at a high-end restaurant or having a specific name-brand clothing. While needs and wants can be somewhat subjective, understanding the difference can keep you from making poor financial decisions. I challenge you to define needs and wants as they relate to your situation. Then, work towards those things you want once you have taken care of your needs.

You are the only one who can decide how and where your money goes. However, planning for your finances is useless without execution. There is discipline involved in implementing this (or any) strategy. Casting a vision for my financial goals and prioritizing how I used money moved me beyond the paycheck-to-paycheck mentality many live in.

Financial strategy does not only apply to the money you earn. As an entrepreneur, you need a way to track the work you do. As my work expanded, I had to make sense of the hours I worked and how much I made, so I used the same bucket strategy for that as well.

Here is how it looks for me:

Ongoing clients. These are clients I work with on a regular basis. I generally work about twenty-five hours a week in this bucket. The money I earn from ongoing clients pays for needs such as ongoing expenses and necessities. Any money left over from this work goes into a savings account that is used for long term financial goals or household expenses.

Project clients. These are the clients who advance my business, but this work ebbs and flows. This work fuels business growth, but does not require long term commitment to the client. I work about fifteen hours a week in this bucket.

Ad hoc or one-off projects. These are the projects that pop up unexpectedly. Since I usually cannot schedule this work in advance, I fit it around ongoing and project work. Sometimes taking on this work requires me to adjust other projects or work extra hours. However, working extra is always weighed against any potential impact to my family. The money in this bucket is used for wants and feeds opportunities for fun and experiences.

Any work assigned to buckets must include expenses that relate to the job. You must have a realistic understanding of what comes in and what goes out. Failing to include the cost of doing business is a big miss and often leads to a rob-Peter-to-pay-Paul financial approach.

The bucket strategy has changed the way I care for finances. When I was young and first started working, I thought about money all the time. Now, I do not think about it all at all. This approach allows me to focus on my actions, rather than the income. It frees up time, helps me stay productive, and encourages me to work towards things on my list. Money no longer has ownership of me; it no longer rules me.

Even with a well-planned strategy, the key is consistency. Consistency is not just about having a routine, though. It is about building momentum by forming habits that lead to success. It fuels growth by setting the stage for expectations for you and your clients. Here is why:

- It helps clients respect your boundaries and prepares them for your availability.
- It helps you stay productive because you know what is needed and when it is needed.
- It frees up mental space by removing clutter caused by distraction. You can focus on the task at hand.
- It increases productivity through repetition. When possible, batch tasks, such as checking email or creating social media content. This approach allows you to become more efficient.

In the end, you must identify the right process for you and the work you do. Find ways to build and continue momentum. For example, I write tasks in a notebook, then tear the page out when I am done. Notebooks are also a great way to catch any random ideas you think of so you can go back later to revisit them.

My biggest takeaway in this process was learning to ask for support. I do not use the word "help" because to me, it implies we are victims. Asking someone to come alongside you and lend a hand is freeing and can be a powerful way to lighten your work. Plus, collaborating with others often breeds new ideas and excitement for what you are doing.

When I was a child and my parents told me to clean my room, I would often call my grandma to come help. Our strategy was to pick everything up off the floor and put it on my bed. Then, she would pick up each item one at a time and ask, "Where does this go?" I often reflect on what she taught me through that process. Looking at my messy room was overwhelming, but by dealing with each item on its own, before we knew it, our work was done.

It is easy to become distracted by the amount of work to do or the need to plan financially, but it does not have to be that way. The message is this: Be consistent, take action, and tackle each item one at a time.

EXAMINE YOUR PATH

Describe the difference between wants and needs.
Where have you allowed your wants to
take precedence over your needs?

2

What specific buckets do you need
to create for your finances?

3

What buckets would best support your workflow?
List them according to priority.

EXECUTE THE ROUTE

Go back to the time inventory in chapter six. What are the top two areas you struggle to be consistent? Map out processes to fit the work in those areas.

Here are some examples:
Create a time schedule for the work: Every Monday do XYZ. Every Tuesday, complete ABC.

Identify ways to make meetings consistent: Schedule follow up meetings on specific days, then limit meeting times.

YOUR SCALE

Every journey includes delays and changes. When you lose momentum,
give yourself permission to start the journey again, and do it often.
~ LEAH MEYERS

PERMISSION TO SOAR

If you travel long enough, you are going to experience a problem
along the way. I never had something happen with my vehicle,
like a flat tire or running out of gas. However, I have had a few
bad travel experiences. I remember once, we were coming home
from Christmas break, and were scheduled to land in Fargo,
North Dakota. Unfortunately, our flight was cancelled. Understand, the upper Midwest is not like flying into a major airport.
It is not always easy to reschedule flights – especially during the
holidays! A cancelled flight can be a nightmare! We were eventually able to switch our flights around and land in Minneapolis,
Minnesota. That trip was so frustrating, I could have sworn off

flying in the winter. Eventually I got over it though, and would make the same trip without hesitation.

In every journey, delays and changes are going to happen and cause us to lose momentum. But do not give up. You gave yourself permission to start the journey and sometimes you must give yourself permission all over again. Start by refocusing on the adventure.

When the road gets uncomfortable or changes, and your mind is filled with reasons to stop, write down your excuses and refute them – just like you did at the beginning. Sometimes you need to challenge what you (or others) say about your journey.

Once I started making headway financially, I knew that I was entering uncharted waters as far as my taxes. By July my second year, I made substantially more than I had the previous year. I knew it was time to meet with a CPA (Certified Public Accountant).

I remember sitting there anxiously as he entered my numbers in his system. When he finished, he looked up at me and said the strangest thing. He said I had two choices. I could keep making money and owe it to Uncle Sam. Or, I could quit working for the rest of the year. If I had not had the confidence to challenge what he said, I would have hung up my laptop and given up. But I knew it was ridiculous advice for me at that time.

In business, there will be times you must reevaluate where you are. His words could have made me question my goal, but it did not. My goal was to be successful financially and his solution did not align with that goal. I had to trust my instinct and give myself permission all over again.

Now understand, if my goal had been to make enough to coast along, this man's words would have made sense, but that was not my vision. There will be moments in your journey when you will have to decide if you are okay with the money you are earning. If you are, it is perfectly fine to go into maintenance mode. This is about finding the right work/life balance for you.

If growth is still part of your vision, you will need to determine what your next best step is. Moments like that are opportunities to reevaluate your strategy. When I had that conversation, I took the time to reexamine my vision. I was meeting my financial goals, but knew long term, it was not about making more money. For me, my next season needed to be about leveraging my skills in a more profound way.

On any journey, there are always opportunities to adjust and change the direction of your journey to meet shifting life goals.

Many times, when people begin working as entrepreneurs, there is a tendency to let the energy that comes from building a business drive them. Then, when they begin to gain momentum and start to reach their goal, their perspective shifts.

Financial success often breeds clarity about long term goals. When stability comes, it is time to reflect on where you have been, celebrate your successes, and reevaluate where you want to go.

Each person's journey will have a different pace. It is okay to shift or adjust the route you are on and to decide if you want to continue or change your current stride. The route you choose can be fast and aggressive, slower and even-paced, or level and sustained. Here are some examples:

- **The level road:** When growth is not your goal, it may be time to coast. This may be the right choice if you have accomplished what you wanted and realize, you are okay where you are.

- **The slight incline road:** When you still want to rise and scale up, you may want to grow at a slower, steady pace. This may be the right choice if you are ready to scale back your efforts and make the journey more controlled.
- **The steep incline road:** When you are okay with your current pace and have additional step goals you want to reach, it may make sense to stay with your current approach. This approach makes sense if you are still in growth mode.

The point is this, you are in control of your dream and your journey. You alone get to choose how much and how hard you want to push yourself.

NOW DREAM EVEN BIGGER

Bigger dreams do not necessarily mean working faster, creating impressive financial portfolios, or amassing a lot of things. I do not believe achievement is about dollar signs; it is about identifying your own version of success. For me, the long-term goal has been about finding a strategy for the long haul.

Stability is different for each person. There are as many variables to this process as there are people. My ongoing dream is about building residual income to free up time and create a scenario where I get to choose what I want to do and when I get to do it. My plan is to build residual income through rental properties and membership opportunities. It is a strategy that will enable me to live the way I want to live.

As you create *your* vision for success, I encourage you to think big and think long-term. Let yourself dream bigger. Imagine the ways you can make that dream a reality. Here are a few questions to get you started:

- What does long-term success look like for me?
- What is my long-term personal goal?
- What is my long-term financial goal?
- How can I prepare now to make my future goals a reality?

MAKE OR BREAK TIME

When you are getting started, you are usually focused on hustling to get to a state of stabilization. It takes discipline to continue at that pace and it is a great accomplishment when you begin to make traction. However, make or break time comes when you reach a level of success. At stabilization, we sometimes fall into traps that can derail long term success. Here are some examples of those mindsets:

- We get bored and boredom often leads to lack of focus and fire.
- We lose motivation, which can cause us to stop or slow down the pace we need to reach our goals.
- We get complacent, which can cause us to get lazy about our work and our goals.
- We start chasing shiny objects. This often results when we become bored, unmotivated, or complacent.
- We allow the demons from our past to creep in and impact how and why we work. Thoughts about our ability to succeed or mindset, such as imposter syndrome,

often surface at stabilization because we are no longer focused on building.

- We start to question when enough is enough. While this is not bad, it can cause us to give up too soon, rather than pushing to a place of true satisfaction.
- We allow ourselves to become undisciplined. Stabilization can become the death of the drive that built many entrepreneurs and businesses.
- We stop believing in our own capabilities. We forget what we did to get where we are and allow ourselves to forget what we have accomplished.

Success requires perseverance, self-confidence, hard work, and a bit of risk taking. However, when stabilization allows the wrong mindsets to creep in, it is time to reset. Remember what you have accomplished and celebrate it.

Know that every journey will require fine tuning. Sometimes things that worked in the past are no longer viable. Maybe your long-term goals have shifted or your vision has changed. Perhaps like me, your *why* has changed. As my kids are growing and getting older, as they start to need me less and less, I am starting to focus on myself and my health. When your vision changes, your journey continues – even though it may look different.

When you reach stabilization, it may be time to ask yourself when enough is enough. Decide if it is time to take the scenic route and enjoy the scenery, instead of racing to get there. When you reach a level of success, give yourself permission to dream even more.

Everyone must face the fact that they will not be young forever. I have spent the last few years building a business and growing towards financial independence. I realize now, it is time to experience new things.

We have many stages in life. At each stage, it is time to re-evaluate and dream bigger. Use the following ideas to get started as you reevaluate:

- Discover a new vision or goal.
- See the beauty in your journey.
- Look for opportunities to enhance your strengths.
- Identify and work through your weaknesses.

In the end, you alone will create what you desire as you throw away your excuses, self-doubt, and fear. What makes someone successful comes from faith in themselves and their willingness to persevere and work hard.

There is great power in acting now. Every journey begins somewhere. It is often a matter of putting the car in drive and placing your foot on the gas pedal.

EXAMINE YOUR PATH

What have you (or others) said about your
journey that may be causing you to hesitate?

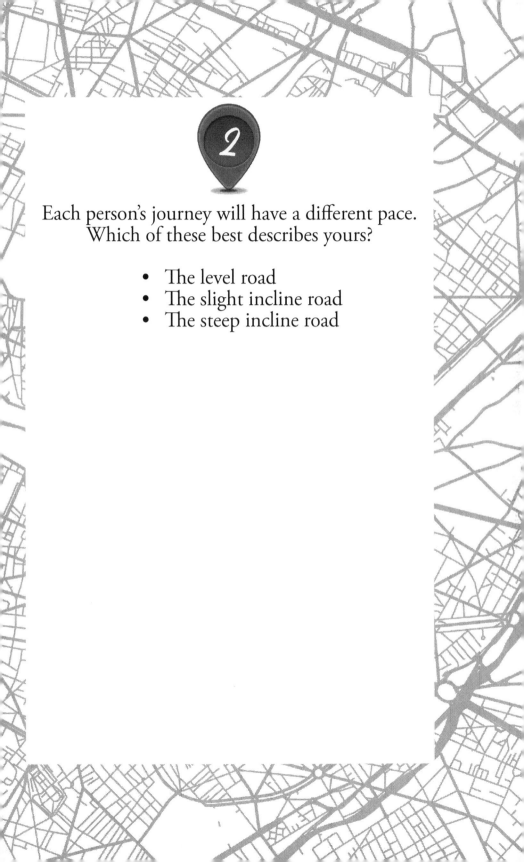

Each person's journey will have a different pace.
Which of these best describes yours?

- The level road
- The slight incline road
- The steep incline road

Go back and review the traps in the section
Make or Break Time.
Which mindset(s) have you fallen into?

EXECUTE THE ROUTE

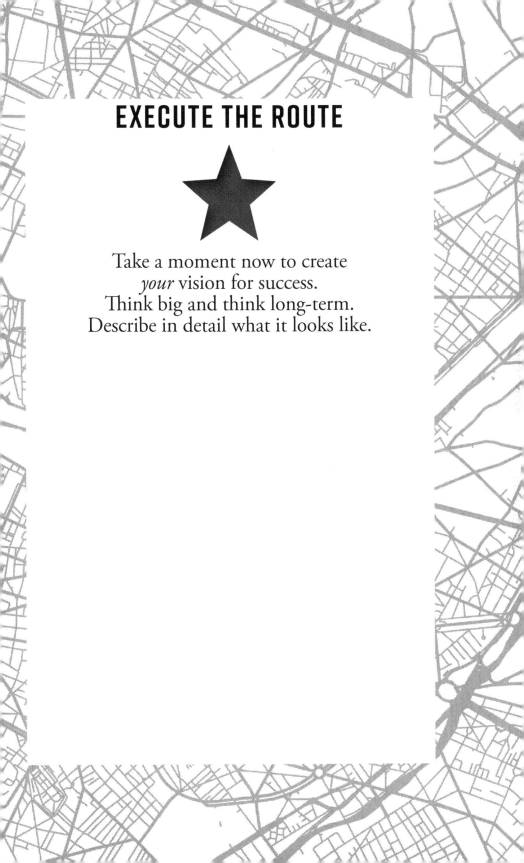

Take a moment now to create
your vision for success.
Think big and think long-term.
Describe in detail what it looks like.

CONCLUSION

As you create your vision for success, I encourage you
to think big and think long-term.

~ LEAH MEYERS

Growing up, my family often traveled around the United States for vacation. My parents were creative in finding resources that allowed us to have experiences we may not otherwise have had. For example, my mother worked at a hotel, which meant we could inexpensively book nice rooms in really nice hotels. I still remember staying on the boardwalk in California. Those experiences showed me the value in using all your resources.

I entered entrepreneurship as a way to make ends meet. However, what began as a job became an opportunity to use the resources I had been honing since I was young. Failed relationships taught me resilience. Rejection taught me to trust my gifts and strengths. Raising kids as a single mom cemented my desire to be a role model for them. Getting rid of black and white thinking gave me the freedom to create my own version of success.

Many times, we view the challenges in our lives as dead ends. We assume that trouble or difficulty is a roadblock to success. Let me tell you, it can be, but it certainly does not have to be that way.

There are countless stories of successful people who have faced down difficulties and risen to success. The problem is, we often read those stories and convince ourselves that those individuals had some secret power or extraordinary skill set that allowed them to get past what life dealt. I can tell you, that belief is simply not true.

Success is not a result of secret power. Every human being faces challenges. However, effective people focus on their vision instead of what is going on around them. They do not get distracted by others' opinions or expectations. And, they find ways to move past failures and doubts.

When I meet someone who says they want success, but struggle to achieve any level of achievement, I know they have allowed their excuses to outweigh their dream. If you want success, you have got to let go of excuses and those things that are not working. It means pressing on towards what you want, even when it feels almost impossible.

Long journeys take focus and determination. The decisions we make over time will always yield results. The question is whether they will be the results you are looking for. If you want positive change, you can…

- Focus on your why.
- Become a forever learner.

- Include fun in the journey.
- Get rid of stinking thinking.
- Allow yourself to be creative.
- Do not be afraid to challenge yourself.
- Get rid of (or limit) distractions.
- Keep your eye on the destination.

Most importantly, you must identify what motivates you. Long term success is about finding and focusing on your why.

Early on, my goal was to be the best role model I could be for my kids. Yes, I wanted to end the financial stress we had experienced. Yes, I wanted to create a legacy that would empower them, and future generations, to find their own vision. But more than that, I wanted to teach my kids the power of earning what you have, embracing their individual strengths and weaknesses, and encouraging them to go after their dreams.

I made the decision to write this book because I have talked to many people who struggle with what it takes to be successful. It is not about learning specific skill sets as much as it is about shifting your mindset. When we change the way we *think* about success, we open ourselves up to new paths and greater possibilities. The battle for success is usually won in our minds!

In the end, it is up to you. You own the choice to succeed and you own the timeline. I have absolute confidence that if you decide you want it, and if you allow yourself to dream it, you can have it. So… what is holding you back from taking the journey of a lifetime?

ABOUT THE AUTHOR

Since her first paid job at sixteen years old, Leah Meyers knew entrepreneurship would be her lifelong calling. For over fifteen years, Leah has coached hundreds of entrepreneurs and small business owners, empowering them to succeed through collaboration. Leah has been a top-rated freelancer on Upwork since 2018. She has consistently earned a six-figure income on Upwork each year since.

Leah knows that the magic that leads to freedom happens when we don't try to go it alone, but when we lean into others and ask others to share their knowledge and wisdom with us.

Leah demonstrates that those who desire transformation can be successful at anything, no matter what. She has the hard-won experience of life-changing achievements to share with anyone who wants to improve their lives.

Made in the USA
Coppell, TX
12 March 2022

74846140R00081